# Harvard Business Review

ON

## SUPPLY CHAIN MANAGEMENT

## THE HARVARD BUSINESS REVIEW PAPERBACK SERIES

The series is designed to bring today's managers and professionals the fundamental information they need to stay competitive in a fast-moving world. From the preeminent thinkers whose work has defined an entire field to the rising stars who will redefine the way we think about business, here are the leading minds and landmark ideas that have established the *Harvard Business Review* as required reading for ambitious businesspeople in organizations around the globe.

**Other books in the series:**

**Other books in the series (continued):**

*Harvard Business Review on Nonprofits*

*Harvard Business Review on Organizational Learning*

*Harvard Business Review on Strategic Alliances*

*Harvard Business Review on Strategies for Growth*

*Harvard Business Review on Teams That Succeed*

*Harvard Business Review on Top-Line Growth*

*Harvard Business Review on Turnarounds*

*Harvard Business Review on Women in Business*

*Harvard Business Review on Work and Life Balance*

# Harvard Business Review

## ON

## SUPPLY CHAIN
## MANAGEMENT

A HARVARD BUSINESS REVIEW PAPERBACK

The *Harvard Business Review* articles in this collection are available as
individual reprints. Discounts apply to quantity purchases. For information and ordering, please contact Customer Service, Harvard Business
School Publishing, Boston, MA 02163. Telephone: (617) 783-7500 or
(800) 988-0886, 8 A.M. to 6 P.M. Eastern Time, Monday through Friday.
Fax: (617) 783-7555, 24 hours a day. E-mail: custserv@hbsp.harvard.edu.

978-1-4221-0279-4 (ISBN 13)

**Library of Congress Cataloging-in-Publication Data**
Harvard business review on supply chain management.
        p.   cm. — (The Harvard business review paperback series)
    Includes index.
    ISBN 1-4221-0279-3
    1. Business logistics.   I. Harvard Business School Press.
II. Harvard business review.   III. Series.
HD38.5.H374 2006
658.7—dc22                                              2006010630

# Contents

# Harvard Business Review

## ON

### SUPPLY CHAIN MANAGEMENT

# We're in This Together

DOUGLAS M. LAMBERT AND

A. MICHAEL KNEMEYER

## Executive Summary

WHEN MANAGERS FROM Wendy's International and Tyson Foods got together in 2003 to craft a supply chain partnership, each side had misgivings. There were those in the Wendy's camp who remembered past disagreements with Tyson and those on the Tyson side who were wary of Wendy's. But the companies had a tool, called the "partnership model," to help get things started on the right foot. Drawing on the experiences of member companies of the Global Supply Chain Forum at Ohio State University, the model offers a process for aligning expectations and determining the most productive level of partnering. It rapidly establishes the mutual understanding and commitment required for success and provides a structure for measuring outcomes. This article puts the tool in the reader's hands.

1

Partnerships are justified only if they stand to yield substantially better results than the firms could achieve on their own. And even if they are warranted, they can fail if the partners enter them with mismatched expectations. Over the course of a day and a half, the partnership model elucidates the drivers behind each company's desire for partnership, allows managers to examine the conditions that facilitate or hamper cooperation, and specifies which activities managers must perform to implement the relationship.

This tool has proved effective at Wendy's and elsewhere in determining what type of partnership is most appropriate. Colgate-Palmolive, for example, used it to help achieve stretch financial goals with suppliers of innovative products. But the model is just as effective in revealing that some companies' visions of partnership are not justified. In matters of the heart, it may be better to have loved and lost, but in business relationships, it's better to have headed off the resource sink and lingering resentments a failed partnership can cause.

---

W HEN MANAGERS FROM Wendy's International and Tyson Foods sat down together in December 2003 to craft a supply chain partnership, each side arrived at the table with misgivings. There were those on the Wendy's side who remembered all too well the disagreements they'd had with Tyson in the past. In fact, just a few years earlier, Wendy's had made a formal decision not to buy from Tyson again. On the Tyson side, some people were wary of a customer whose demands had prevented the business from meeting its profit goals.

A few things had changed in the meantime, or the companies wouldn't have been at the table at all. First, the menu at Wendy's had shifted with consumer tastes—chicken had become just as important as beef. The restaurant chain had a large-volume chicken supplier, but it wanted to find yet another. Second, Tyson had acquired leading beef supplier IBP, with which Wendy's had a strong relationship. IBP's president and COO, Richard Bond, now held the positions of president and COO of the combined organization, so Wendy's felt it had someone it could work with at Tyson.

One other thing had changed, too. The companies had a new tool, called the partnership model, to help start the relationship off on the right foot. Developed under the auspices of Ohio State University's Global Supply Chain Forum, the model incorporated lessons learned from the best partnering experiences of that group's 15 member companies. It offered a process for aligning expectations and determining the level of cooperation that would be most productive.

With this article, we put that tool in your hands. We'll explain how, over the course of a day and a half, it illuminates the drivers behind each company's desire for partnership, allows managers to examine the conditions that facilitate or hamper cooperation, and specifies which activities managers in the two companies must perform, and at what level, to implement the partnership. The model—proven at Wendy's and in dozens of other partnership efforts—rapidly establishes the mutual understanding and commitment required for success and provides a structure for measuring outcomes. (See the exhibit "The Partnership Model" for a graphical depiction.)

# No Partnership for Its Own Sake

Why do so many partnerships fail to deliver value? Often it's because they shouldn't have existed in the first place. Partnerships are costly to implement—they

---

### The Partnership Model

*When the member companies of the Global Supply Chain Forum first convened in 1992, they agreed they needed insights on how to build effective partnerships. Research on their experiences formed the basis of a model that has been refined through dozens of partnership facilitation sessions. Managers state the drivers behind their desire to partner and examine the conditions that would facilitate cooperation. The model helps them decide on a partnership type and boost the needed managerial components. Later, if the partners aren't happy with the relationship, they determine whether drivers or facilitators have changed or components are at an appropriate level.*

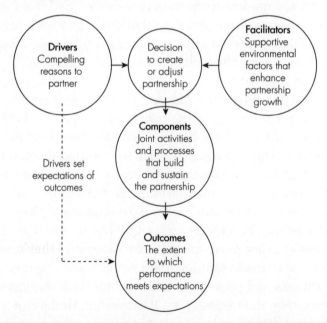

---

*Diagram source: Douglas M. Lambert, Margaret A. Emmelhainz, and John T. Gardner, "So You Think You Want a Partner?" Marketing Management, Summer 1996.*

require extra communication, coordination, and risk sharing. They are justified only if they stand to yield substantially better results than the firms could achieve without partnering.

This point was driven home for us early in our research with the Global Supply Chain Forum when its members identified successful partnerships for study. One was an arrangement between a package delivery company and a manufacturer. The delivery company got the revenue it had been promised, and the manufacturer got the cost and service levels that had been stipulated. But it wasn't a partnership; it was a single-source contract with volume guaranteed. The point is that it's often possible to get the results you want without a partnership. If that's the case, don't create one. Just write a good contract. You simply don't have enough human resources to form tight relationships with every supplier or customer.

At Wendy's, managers distinguish between high- and low-value partnership opportunities using a two-by-two matrix with axes labeled "complexity to Wendy's" and "volume of the buy." Supplies such as drinking straws might be purchased in huge volumes, but they present no complexities in terms of taste, texture, or safety. Only if both volume and complexity are high—as with key ingredients—does Wendy's seek a partnership. Colgate-Palmolive similarly plots suppliers on a matrix according to "potential for cost reductions" and "potential for innovation" and explores partnering opportunities with those that rank high in both.

Reserving partnerships for situations where they're justified is one way to ensure they deliver value. Even then, however, they can fail if partners enter into them with mismatched expectations. Like the word "commitment" in a marriage, "partnership" can be interpreted quite differently by the parties involved—and both sides often are so certain that their interpretations are shared that their assumptions are never articulated or questioned.

What's needed, then, for supply chain partnerships to succeed is a way of targeting high-potential relationships and aligning expectations around them. This is what the partnership model is designed to do. It is not designed to be a supplier-selection tool. At Wendy's, for instance, the model was employed only after the company's senior vice president of supply chain management, Judy Hollis, had reduced the company's supplier base, consolidating to 225 suppliers. At that point, Wendy's could say: "Now the decision's been made. You're a supplier. Your business isn't at risk. What we're trying to do here is structure the relationship so we get the most out of it for the least amount of effort." That assurance helped people to speak more frankly about their hopes for the partnership—an absolute necessity for the partnership-building process to succeed.

## A Forum for Frank Discussion

Under the model, key representatives of two potential partners come together for a day and a half to focus solely on the partnership. Little preparatory work is required of them, but the same can't be said for the meeting's organizers (usually staff people from the company that has initiated the process). The organizers face a number of important tasks before the session. First, they must find a suitable location, preferably off-site for both parties. Second, they must engage a session leader. It doesn't work to have someone who is associated with one of the companies, as we know from the experience of forum members. We recall one session in particular run by Don Jablonski of Masterfoods USA's purchasing operation. Don is an all-around good guy, is very able at running sessions, and was familiar with the model, but the supplier's people clammed up and the session went nowhere. They needed an outsider.

Third, the organizers must do some calendar juggling to ensure that the right people attend on both sides. Though there is no magic number of representatives, each team should include a broad mix of managers and individuals with functional expertise. The presence of high-level executives ensures that the work won't be second-guessed, and middle managers, operations people, and staff personnel from departments such as HR, finance, and marketing can provide valuable perspectives on the companies' expected day-to-day interactions.

## Goals in the Cold Light of Day

After introductions and an overview, the morning of the first day is consumed by the "drivers session," in which each side's team considers a potential partnership in terms of "What's in it for us?" (See "How to Commit in 28 Hours" at the end of this article.)

The teams are separated in two rooms, and each is asked to discuss and then list the compelling reasons, from its point of view, for a partnership. It's vital that participants feel free to speak frankly about whether and how their own company could benefit from such a relationship. What are the potential payoffs? For some teams, there aren't many. Other teams fill page after page of flip charts.

The partnership drivers fall into four categories—asset and cost efficiencies, customer service enhancements, marketing advantages, and profit growth or stability. The session leader and the provided forms ensure that each of these categories is explicitly addressed. For example, under asset and cost efficiencies, a team might specify desired savings in product costs, distribution, packaging, or information handling. The goal is for the participants to build specific bullet-point descriptions for each driver category with metrics and targets. For the session leader, whose job is to get the teams to articulate measurable goals, this may be the toughest part of the day. It isn't enough for a team to say that the company is looking for "improved asset utilization" or "product cost savings." The goals must be specific, such as improving utilization from 80% to 98% or cutting product costs by 7% per year.

Next, the teams use a five-point scale (1 being "no chance" and 5 being "certain") to rate the likelihood that the partnership will deliver the desired results in each of the four major categories. An extra point is awarded (raising the score to as high as 6) if the result would yield a sustainable competitive advantage by matching or exceeding the industry benchmark in that area. The scores are added (the highest possible score is 24) to produce a total driver score for each side.

This is the point at which the day gets interesting. The teams reassemble in one room and present their drivers and scores to each other. The rules of the game are made clear. If one side doesn't understand how the other's goals would be met, it must push for clarification. Failure to challenge a driver implies agreement and obligates the partners to cooperate on it. The drivers listed by a Wendy's supplier, for instance, included the prospect of doing more business with the Canadian subsidiary of Wendy's, Tim Hortons. The Wendy's team rejected the driver, explaining that the subsidiary's management made decisions autonomously. This is just the sort of expectation that is left unstated in most partnerships and later becomes a source of disappointment.

But expectations are adjusted upward as often as they are lowered. On several occasions, managers reacting to a drivers presentation have been pleasantly surprised to discover a shared goal that hadn't been raised earlier because both sides had assumed it wouldn't fly with the other.

The drivers session is invaluable in getting everyone's motivations onto the table and calibrating the two sides' expectations. It also offers a legitimate forum for discussing contentious issues or clearing the air on past grievances. During one Wendy's session, the discussion veered off on a very useful tangent about why the company's specifications were costly to meet. In another memorable session, we heard a manager on the buying side of a relationship say, "I feel like this is a marriage that's reached the point where you don't think I'm as beautiful as I used to be." His counterpart snapped: "Well, maybe you're not the woman I married anymore." The candor of the subsequent discussion allowed the two sides to refocus on what they could gain by working together. As Judy Hollis told us about the Wendy's-Tyson session, "What they presented to us during the sharing of drivers confirmed that we could have a deeper relationship with them. If we had seen things that were there just to please us, we wouldn't have been willing to go forward with a deeper relationship."

## The Search for Compatibility

Once the two sides have reached agreement on the business results they hope to achieve, the focus shifts to the organizational environment in which the partnership would function. In a new session, the two sides jointly consider the extent to which they believe certain key factors that we call "facilitators" are in place to support the venture. The four most important are compatibility of corporate cultures, compatibility of management philosophy and techniques, a strong sense of mutuality, and symmetry between the two parties. The group, as a whole, is asked to score—again, on a five-point scale—the facilitators' perceived strengths. (This implies, of course, that the participants have a history of interaction on which to draw. If the relationship is new, managers will need to spend some time working on joint projects before they can attempt this assessment.)

For culture and for management philosophy and techniques, the point is not to look for sameness. Partners needn't have identical cultures or management approaches; some differences are benign. Instead, participants are asked to consider differences that are bound to create problems. Does one company's management push decision making down into the organization while the other's executives issue orders from on high? Is one side committed to continuous improvement and the other not? Are people compensated in conflicting ways? The session leader must counter the groups' natural tendency to paint too rosy a picture of how well the organizations would mesh. He or she can accomplish this by asking for an example to illustrate any cultural or management similarity participants may cite. Once the example is on the table, someone in the room will often counter it by saying, "Yeah, but they also do *this* . . ."

A sense of mutuality—of shared purpose and perspective—is vital. It helps the organizations move beyond a zero-sum mentality and respect the spirit of partnership, even if the earnings of one partner are under pressure. It may extend to a willingness to integrate systems or share certain financial information. Symmetry often means comparable scale, industry position, or brand image. But even if two companies are quite dissimilar in these respects, they might assign themselves a high score on symmetry if they hold equal power over each other's marketplace success—perhaps because the smaller company supplies a component that is unique, in scarce supply, or critical to the larger company's competitive advantage.

Beyond these four major facilitators, five others remain to be assessed: shared competitors, physical proximity, potential for exclusivity, prior relationship experience, and shared end users. Each can add one point to the total, for a maximum facilitator score of 25. These factors won't cripple a partnership if they are absent, but where they are present, they deepen the connection. Think of the extra closeness it must have given the McDonald's and Coke partnership in the 1990s that both companies loved to hate Pepsi (which at the time owned Kentucky Fried Chicken, Taco Bell, and Pizza Hut franchises, giving it more locations than McDonald's). Physical proximity certainly adds a dimension to the partnership Wendy's has with sauce supplier T. Marzetti. With both headquarters in Columbus, Ohio, the two companies' R&D staffs can collaborate easily. We saw the benefits of proximity, too, in 3M and Target's partnership. Twin Cities-based managers accustomed to interacting through local charities, arts organizations, and community-building efforts found it easy to collaborate in their work.

Assessing these issues carefully and accurately is worth the sometimes considerable effort, because the scores on facilitators and on drivers in the first session yield a prescription for partnering. The exhibit "The Propensity-to-Partner Matrix" shows how the scores indicate which type of association would be best—a Type I, II, or III partnership or simply an arm's-length relationship. The types entail varying levels of managerial complexity and resource use. In Type I, the organizations recognize each other as partners and coordinate activities and planning on a limited basis. In Type II, the companies integrate activities involving multiple divisions and functions. In Type III, they share a significant level of integration, with each viewing the other as an extension of itself. Type III partnerships are equivalent, in alliance terminology, to strategic alliances, but we are careful to avoid such value-laden language because there should be no implication that more integration is better than less integration.

To put this in perspective, recall that Wendy's began by consolidating its buying to 225 suppliers. Of these, only the top 40 are being taken through the partnership-model process. And it appears that only a few of the partnerships will end up being Type III. Perhaps 12 or 15 will be Type II, and about 20 will be Type I. This feels like an appropriate distribution. We don't want participants aspiring to Type III partnerships. We simply want them to fit the type of relationship to the business situation and the organizational environment.

Naturally, the managers in the room do not have to simply accept the prescription. If the outcome surprises them in any way, it may well be time for a reality check. They should ask themselves: "Is it reasonable to commit the resources for this type of partnership, given what we know of our drivers and the facilitators?" If the answer is in doubt, the final session of the process, focusing on the

## The Propensity-to-Partner Matrix

*What type of partnership would be best? Once they have measured their desire to partner and determined how easily they could coordinate activities, companies considering working together can use this matrix to decide whether to form a partnership and, if so, at what level.*

| Ease of Coordination (measured by "facilitator points") | Companies' desire for partnership (measured by "driver points") | | |
|---|---|---|---|
| | 8–11 | 12–15 | 16–24 |
| 16–25 | | | Best partnership type: **III**, in which each company views the other as an extension of itself |
| 12–15 | | Best partnership type: **II**, in which activities of multiple divisions are integrated | |
| 8–11 | Best partnership type: **I**, in which coordination is limited | | |
| | Best type of relationship: **arm's-length** | | |

managerial requirements of the partnership, will clarify matters.

## Action Items and Time Frames

In the third session, the group reconvenes as a whole to focus on management components—the joint activities and processes required to launch and sustain the partnership. While drivers and facilitators determine which type of relationship would be best, management components are the building blocks of partnership. They include capabilities for planning, joint operating controls, communication, and risk/reward sharing. They are universal across firms and across business environments and, unlike drivers and facilitators, are under the direct control of the managers involved.

The two teams jointly develop action plans to put these components in place at a level that is appropriate for the partnership type. Participants are provided with a table of components, listed in order of importance (a portion of such a table is shown in the exhibit "Management Components for Partnerships"). The first task is for the teams to determine the degree to which the components are already in place. This is a quick process; the participants run through the components in the table, noting whether each type of activity is performed at a high, medium, or low level. Generally speaking, the components should be at a high level for Type III partnerships, a medium level for Type II, and a low level for Type I.

Under the heading of joint operating controls, for example, a Type III partnership would call for developing performance measures jointly and focusing those measures on the companies' combined performance. A Type II partnership, by contrast, would involve performance measures that focus on each company's individual performance, regardless of how well the partner performs. In a Type I partnership, the companies would not work together to develop mutually satisfactory performance measures, though they might share their results.

For each management component, the group must outline what, if anything, needs to be done to move from the current state to the capability level required by the partnership. Here, it is helpful to refocus on the drivers agreed to in session one and start developing action plans around each of them. It is in these action plans that the deficiencies of the current management components become apparent. It may be, for instance, that achieving a particular goal depends on systematic joint planning, but the group has just said planning is being performed at a low level. Clearly, planning must be ratcheted up.

One of the needs that became clear in the Tyson-Wendy's session was for increased communication at the upper levels. People at the operational level in the two companies were communicating regularly and effectively, but there was no parallel for that at the top. Joe Gordon, a commodity manager at Wendy's, explained why this was a problem: "All of us worker bees sometimes come to a point where we have obstacles in our day-to-day relationship, and in the past we might have given up on trying to overcome them." After an action plan was outlined for getting the top management teams together to talk, those problems became easier to address.

When the participants leave, they leave with action items, time frames for carrying them out, and a designation of responsible parties. The fact that so much is accomplished in such a brief period is a source of

## Management Components for Partnerships*

| Partnership Component | Low | Medium | High |
|---|---|---|---|
| **Planning:** | | | |
| • Style | • on ad hoc basis | • regularly scheduled | • systematic: both scheduled and ad hoc |
| • Level | • focus is on projects or tasks | • focus is on process | • focus is on relationship |
| • Content | • sharing of existing plans | • performed jointly, eliminating conflicts in strategies | • performed jointly and at multiple levels, including top management; each party participates in other's business planning |
| **Joint Operating Controls:** | | | |
| • Measurement | • performance measures are developed independently, but results might be shared | • measures are jointly developed and shared; focus is on individual firm's performance | • measures are jointly developed and shared; focus is on relationship and joint performance |
| • Ability to make changes | • parties may suggest changes to other's system | • parties may make changes to other's system after getting approval | • parties may make changes to other's system without getting approval |

**Communication:**

| | | | |
|---|---|---|---|
| Nonroutine | • very limited, usually just critical issues at the task or project level | • conducted more regularly, done at multiple levels; generally open and honest | • planned as part of the relationship; occurs at all levels; sharing of praise and criticism; parties "speak the same language" |
| **Day-to-day** | | | |
| • Organization | • conducted on ad hoc basis, between individuals | • limited number of scheduled communications; some routinization | • systematized method of communication; communication systems are linked |
| • Balance | • primarily one-way | • two-way but unbalanced | • balanced two-way communication flow |
| • Electronic | • use of individual systems | • joint modification of individual systems | • joint development of customized electronic communications |

**Risk/Reward Sharing:**

| | | | |
|---|---|---|---|
| • Loss tolerance | • very low tolerance for loss | • some tolerance for short-term loss | • high tolerance for short-term loss |
| • Gain commitment | • limited willingness to help the other gain | • willingness to help the other gain | • desire to help other party gain |
| • Commitment to fairness | • fairness is evaluated by transaction | • fairness is tracked year to year | • fairness is measured over life of relationship |

*In general, Type III partnerships require high levels of most of these components, Type II partnerships require medium levels, and Type I relationships require low levels. (This is just a partial list of managerial components.)

continued motivation. Donnie King, who heads Tyson's poultry operations, admitted that he had been skeptical going into the meeting. "You tend to believe it is going to be a process where you sit around the campfire and hold hands and sing 'Kumbaya' and nothing changes," he said. But when he left the meeting, he knew there would be change indeed.

## A Versatile Tool

The current quality of interaction and cooperation between Tyson Foods and Wendy's International suggests that the partnership model is effective not only in designing new relationships but also in turning around troubled ones. Today, Wendy's buys heavily from Tyson and believes the partnership produces value similar to that of the other Wendy's key-ingredient partnerships. Richard Bond of Tyson told us: "There is a greater level of trust between the two companies. We have had a higher level of involvement in QA regulations and how our plants are audited [by Wendy's], rather than having [those processes] dictated to us."

The two companies' R&D and marketing groups have begun to explore new products that would allow Wendy's to expand its menu, with Tyson as a key supplier. In a recent interview, we asked the director of supply chain management for Wendy's, Tony Scherer, to recall the tense conversations of the December 2003 partnership session, and we wondered whether that history still colored the relationship. "No," he said. "I really do feel like we've dropped it now, and we can move on."

For other companies, the partnership model has paid off in different ways. Colgate-Palmolive used it to help achieve stretch financial goals with key suppliers of inno-

vative products. TaylorMade-adidas Golf Company used
it to structure supplier relationships in China. At International Paper, the model helped to align expectations
between two divisions that supply each other and have
distinct P&Ls. And it served Cargill well when the company wanted several of its divisions, all dealing separately with Masterfoods USA, to present a more unified
face to the customer. The session was unwieldy, with
seven Cargill groups interacting with three Masterfoods
divisions, but the give-and-take yielded a wide range of
benefits, from better utilization of a Cargill cocoa plant
in Brazil to more effective hedging of commodity price
risk at Masterfoods.

But to focus only on these success stories is to miss
much of the point of the model. Just as valuable, we
would argue, are the sessions in which participants discover that their vision of partnership is not justified by
the benefits it can reasonably be expected to yield. In
matters of the heart, it may be better to have loved and
lost, but in business relationships, it's far better to have
avoided the resource sink and lingering resentments of a
failed partnership. Study the relationships that have
ended up as disappointments to one party or both, and
you will find a common theme: mismatched and unreal-
istic expectations. Executives in each firm were using the
same word, "partnership," but envisioning different relationships. The partnership model ensures that both parties see the opportunity wholly and only for what it is.

# How to Commit in 28 Hours

### Before the Meeting

A CROSS-FUNCTIONAL, multilevel team from each company is identified and commits to a meeting time. A location is found, preferably off-site for both parties.

### Day One
### Morning

**Introductions and an Overview.** The session leader explains the rationale for using the model.

**Articulation of Drivers.** The two teams meet separately to discuss why they are seeking a partnership and to list specific, selfish reasons in four categories: asset and cost efficiencies, customer service improvements, marketing advantages, and profit growth or stability. A score is assigned to each category, indicating the likelihood that the partnership would serve those goals.

### Afternoon

**Presentation of Drivers.** The groups present their drivers to each other. Each team must challenge every driver it considers unsupportable or unacceptable. Failure to challenge a goal implies agreement and obligates the organization to help the potential partner achieve the aim. The teams also compare driver scores. The lower of the two becomes the driver score for the proposed partnership (that's because the less motivated team is the relationship's limiting factor).

**Evaluation of Facilitators.** The teams jointly examine the features of the shared organizational environment that would help or hinder cooperation. Scores are assigned to four basic and five additional factors.

**Prescription of Partnership Level.** The group consults the propensity-to-partner matrix, which yields a prescription based on the scores. The ideal relationship looks like a Type I, II, or III partnership or simply an arm's-length association.

## Day Two

## Morning

**Examination of Components.** The group examines the management components required for the level of partnership prescribed by the matrix and considers to what extent those components currently exist on both sides. A plan is made for developing needed components. The plans include specific actions, responsible parties, and due dates.

**Review.** The drivers articulated on day one are reviewed to ensure that each has been targeted with specific action plans.

**Originally published December 2004**
**Reprint R0412H**

# Building Deep Supplier Relationships

JEFFREY K. LIKER AND THOMAS Y. CHOI

## Executive Summary

MORE AND MORE BUSINESSES ARE counting on their
suppliers to lower costs, improve quality, and develop
innovations faster than their competitors' suppliers can.
To this end, many experts agree that American firms, like
their Japanese rivals, should build supplier *keiretsu:* networks of vendors that learn, improve, and prosper in
sync with their parent companies.

As history has shown, however, that's easier said than
done. Some U.S. corporations created supply chains
that superficially resembled those of their Japanese competitors, but they didn't alter the nature of their relationships with suppliers. As a result, relations between U.S.
manufacturers and their suppliers have sunk to the lowest
levels in decades.

But reports of keiretsu's demise are overblown. The
Japanese supplier-partnering model is alive and well—in

North America as well as Japan. During the past ten years, automakers Toyota and Honda have struck successful partnerships with some of the same suppliers that are at odds with the Big Three and created effective keiretsu across Canada, the United States, and Mexico.

So how do Toyota and Honda do it? The authors, who have studied the American and Japanese automobile industries for more than 20 years, found that Toyota and Honda have built great supplier relationships by following six steps. First, they understand how their suppliers work. Second, they turn supplier rivalry into opportunity. Third, they monitor vendors closely. Fourth, they develop those vendors' capabilities. Fifth, they share information intensively but selectively. And sixth, they help their vendors continually improve their processes.

Toyota and Honda succeed because they consistently follow all six directives. Thus, the automakers have not only stayed in the game with the Big Three but have also redefined the playing field.

---

*"The Big Three [U.S. automakers] set annual cost-reduction targets [for the parts they purchase]. To realize those targets, they'll do anything. [They've unleashed] a reign of terror, and it gets worse every year. You can't trust anyone [in those companies]."*
—DIRECTOR, INTERIOR SYSTEMS SUPPLIER TO FORD, GM, AND CHRYSLER, OCTOBER 1999

*"Honda is a demanding customer, but it is loyal to us. [American] automakers have us work on drawings, ask other suppliers to bid on them, and give the job to the lowest bidder. Honda never does that."*
—CEO, INDUSTRIAL FASTENERS SUPPLIER TO FORD, GM, CHRYSLER, AND HONDA, APRIL 2002

*"In my opinion, [Ford] seems to send its people to 'hate school' so that they learn how to hate suppliers. The company is extremely confrontational. After dealing with Ford, I decided not to buy its cars."*
—SENIOR EXECUTIVE, SUPPLIER TO FORD, OCTOBER 2002

*"Toyota helped us dramatically improve our production system. We started by making one component, and as we improved, [Toyota] rewarded us with orders for more components. Toyota is our best customer."*
—SENIOR EXECUTIVE, SUPPLIER TO FORD, GM, CHRYSLER, AND TOYOTA, JULY 2001

No CORPORATION NEEDS TO BE convinced that in today's scale-driven, technology-intensive global economy, partnerships are the supply chain's lifeblood. Companies, especially in developed economies, buy more components and services from suppliers than they used to. The 100 biggest U.S. manufacturers spent 48 cents out of every dollar of sales in 2002 to buy materials, compared with 43 cents in 1996, according to *Purchasing* magazine's estimates. Businesses are increasingly relying on their suppliers to reduce costs, improve quality, and develop new processes and products faster than their rivals' vendors can. In fact, some organizations have started to evaluate whether they must continue to assemble products themselves or whether they can outsource production entirely. The issue isn't whether companies should turn their arm's-length relationships with suppliers into close partnerships, but how. Happily, the advice on that score is quite consistent: Experts agree that American corporations, like their Japanese rivals, should build supplier *keiretsu:* close-knit networks of vendors that continuously learn, improve, and prosper along with their parent companies. (Incidentally, we don't mean that companies should create complex cross holdings of shares between themselves and their suppliers, the way Japanese firms do.)

For corporations intimidated by the prospect of building familial ties with the suppliers they've traditionally bullied, our research offers some bad news and some good news. First, the bad news: It's tougher to build relationships with suppliers than companies imagine. For more than 20 years, many American businesses have unsuccessfully tried to build bonds with suppliers. As part of the quality movement of the 1980s, these companies ostensibly adopted the Japanese partnering model. They slashed the number of suppliers they did business with, awarded the survivors long-term contracts, and encouraged top-tier vendors to manage the lower tiers. They also got top-tier suppliers to produce subsystems instead of components, to take responsibility for quality and costs, and to deliver just in time. In 2001, the Malcolm Baldrige National Quality Award Committee made "key supplier and customer partnering and communication mechanisms" a separate category on which it would judge the best companies in the United States.

However, while these American companies created supply chains that superficially resembled those of their Japanese competitors, they didn't alter the fundamental nature of their relationships with suppliers. It wasn't long into the partnering movement before manufacturers and suppliers were fighting bitterly over the implementation of best practices like continuous quality improvement and annual price reductions. By the turn of the millennium, two additional factors made cost, again, the main criterion in supplier selection. First, companies were more easily able to source globally, notably from

China. They jumped to the conclusion that the immediate benefits of low wage costs outweighed the long-term benefits of investing in relationships. Second, the development and spread of Internet-based technologies allowed companies to get suppliers to compete on cost more efficiently—and more brutally—than they used to. Consequently, manufacturer-supplier relations in America have deteriorated so much that they're worse now than before the quality revolution began. In the U.S. automobile industry, for instance, Ford uses online reverse auctions to get the lowest prices for components. GM writes contracts that allow it to shift to a less expensive supplier at a moment's notice. Chrysler tried to build a keiretsu, but the process unraveled after Daimler took over the company in 1998. Not surprisingly, the Big Three have been more or less at war with their suppliers. Having witnessed the American automakers' abject failure to create keiretsu, most Western companies doubt they can replicate the model outside the culture and society of Japan.

Time, perhaps, for the good news. Contrary to the cynics' beliefs, the reports of the keiretsu's demise are greatly exaggerated. The Japanese supplier-partnering model is alive, well, and flourishing—not just in Japan but also in North America. During the past decade, $160 billion Toyota and $75 billion Honda have struck remarkable partnerships with some of the same suppliers that are at loggerheads with the Big Three and have created latter-day keiretsu across Canada, the United States, and Mexico. The two Japanese companies work closely with their suppliers in those areas. Of the 2.1 million Toyota/Lexus vehicles and the 1.6 million Honda/Acura vehicles sold in North America in 2003, Toyota manufactured 60% and Honda produced 80% in

North America. Moreover, the two companies source about 70% to 80% of the costs of making each automobile from North American suppliers. Despite the odds, Toyota and Honda have managed to replicate in an alien Western culture the same kind of supplier webs they built in Japan. Consequently, they enjoy the best supplier relations in the U.S. automobile industry, have the fastest product development processes, and reduce costs and improve quality year after year. Consider the evidence:

- In 2003, when Planning Perspective, a Birmingham, Michigan–based research company, conducted the OEM Benchmark Survey, one of the principal measures of manufacturer-supplier relations in the U.S. automobile industry, it rated Toyota and Honda as the most preferred companies to work with. In 17 categories, ranging from trust to perceived opportunity, Toyota and Honda led. They were followed by Nissan, while Chrysler, Ford, and GM were a distant fourth, fifth, and sixth. In particular, suppliers said that Toyota and Honda were better communicators and that they were more trustworthy and more concerned about suppliers' profitability than other manufacturers were.

- While U.S. automakers take two to three years to design new cars, Toyota and Honda have consistently been able to do so in just 12 to 18 months. Last year, a J.D. Power and Associates study found that suppliers rated Toyota among the best and rated Honda above average at promoting innovation. The study found that Chrysler, Ford, and GM were below average at fostering innovation with vendors.

- According to several academic papers, Toyota and Honda brought down the manufacturing costs of the

Camry and the Accord by about 25% during the 1990s. Still, the two companies have appeared at the top of surveys by J.D. Power and Associates and Consumer Reports on initial quality and long-term durability. They also produced the most reliable cars and recalled fewer vehicles in the United States in the past ten years than GM, Ford, or Chrysler did.

Just how do Toyota and Honda get it right when their rivals get it so wrong? We have been studying the American and Japanese automobile industries for more than two decades. Between 1999 and 2002, we interviewed more than 50 Toyota and Honda managers in Japan and the United States, several executives who had left those companies' American subsidiaries, and managers from more than 40 suppliers in the North American automobile industry. We also visited Toyota and Honda plants in the United States, suppliers' factories and technical centers, the Toyota Technical Center in Ann Arbor, Michigan, and Honda of America's Purchasing Office in Marysville, Ohio. Our research shows that Toyota and Honda have developed partnerships with their American suppliers by following similar approaches.

## Tough Love

When Toyota and Honda set up manufacturing operations in North America in the 1980s, they started by encouraging the creation of some joint ventures between their Japanese suppliers and American companies. Later, they selected local companies they could develop as suppliers. They gave their new vendors small orders to begin with and expected them to meet certain cost, quality, and delivery parameters. If suppliers coped with the first orders well, Toyota and Honda awarded them larger contracts and taught them their "ways" of doing business. (For more on these approaches, see Jeffrey K. Liker's book, *The Toyota Way: 14 Management Principles from the World's Greatest Manufacturer* and *Powered by Honda: Developing Excellence in the Global Enterprise,* by Dave Nelson, Rick Mayo, and Patricia E. Moody.)

When we compared the elements of Toyota's partnering model with those of Honda's, we found that although the two companies used different tools, they had created strikingly similar scaffoldings. Experts usually emphasize the use of devices like target pricing, but we believe Toyota and Honda have built great supplier relationships by following six distinct steps: First, they understand how their suppliers work. Second, they turn supplier rivalry into opportunity. Third, they supervise their vendors. Fourth, they develop their suppliers' technical capabilities. Fifth, they share information intensively but selectively. And sixth, they conduct joint improvement activities. Some of these steps support others. For example, if manufacturers deploy controls without creating a foundation of understanding, that will lead to gaming behavior by suppliers. We therefore organized the six steps as a supplier-partnering hierarchy, with one leading to the next. Toyota and Honda have succeeded not because they use one or two of these elements but because they use all six together as a system. (See the exhibit "The Supplier-Partnering Hierarchy.")

Most vendors believe that Toyota and Honda are their best—and toughest—customers. The two companies set high standards and expect their partners to rise to meet them. However, the carmakers help suppliers fulfill those expectations. Clearly, Toyota and Honda want to maximize profits, but not at the expense of their suppliers. As Taiichi Ohno, who created the Toyota Production

## The Supplier-Partnering Hierarchy

**Conduct joint improvement activities.**
• Exchange best practices with suppliers.
• Initiate *kaizen* projects at suppliers' facilities.
• Set up supplier study groups.

**Share information intensively but selectively.**
• Set specific times, places, and agendas for meetings.
• Use rigid formats for sharing information.
• Insist on accurate data collection.
• Share information in a structured fashion.

**Develop suppliers' technical capabilities.**
• Build suppliers' problem-solving skills.
• Develop a common lexicon.
• Hone core suppliers' innovation capabilities.

**Supervise your suppliers.**
• Send monthly report cards to core suppliers.
• Provide immediate and constant feedback.
• Get senior managers involved in solving problems.

**Turn supplier rivalry into opportunity.**
• Source each component from two or three vendors.
• Create compatible production philosophies and systems.
• Set up joint ventures with existing suppliers to transfer knowledge and maintain control.

**Understand how your suppliers work.**
• Learn about suppliers' businesses.
• Go see how suppliers work.
• Respect suppliers' capabilities.
• Commit to coprosperity.

System, has said, "The achievement of business performance by the parent company through bullying suppliers
is totally alien to the spirit of the Toyota Production System." The key word in that statement is "parent," which
signals a long-term relationship that involves trust and
mutual well-being. At the same time, the relationship
connotes discipline and the expectation of improvement
and growth. Take, for example, Toyota's Construction of
Cost Competitiveness for the 21st Century (CCC21) program, which aims at a 30% reduction in the prices of 170
parts that the company will buy for its next generation of
vehicles. During our interviews, we didn't hear vendors
decrying CCC21 as unfair. Instead, they wanted to give
Toyota the price reductions it sought. They believed Toyota would help them achieve that target by making their
manufacturing processes leaner, and because of Toyota's
tough love, they would become more competitive—and
more profitable—in the future.

## Understand How Your Suppliers Work

*"Whenever I ask [executives in the Big Three] how they
developed a target price, the answer is: silence. They base
the target price on nothing. The finance manager just
divvies up the available money: 'Here's what we normally
spend on braking systems, here's what you'll get this year.'
They have no idea how we'll get those cost reductions. They
just want them."*
    —Senior Executive, brake-lining supplier to U.S.
       automakers, February 2002

Unlike most companies we know, Toyota and Honda
take the trouble to learn all they can about their suppliers. They believe they can create the foundations for

partnerships only if they know as much about their vendors as the vendors know about themselves. They don't
cut corners while figuring out the operations and cultures of the firms they do business with. Toyota uses the
terms *genchi genbutsu* or *gemba* (actual location and
actual parts or materials) to describe the practice of
sending executives to see and understand for themselves
how suppliers work. Honda uses a similar approach, and
both companies insist that managers at all levels—right
up to their presidents—study suppliers firsthand to
understand them.

The process can take a while, but it usually proves to
be valuable for both the suppliers and the manufacturers. In 1987, when Honda of America was toying with
the idea of using Atlantic Tool and Die as a source for
stamping and welding jobs, it sent one of its engineers to
spend a year with the Cleveland-based company. For 12
months, the middle manager studied the way the organization worked, collected data and facts, and informally
shared the findings with his counterparts at Atlantic.
Over time, they agreed with the Honda engineer's con-
clusions and implemented many of his suggestions,
which led to marked improvements on the shop floor.
About six months into his stay, the Honda engineer
asked Atlantic's top managers to show him the company's books, which they reluctantly agreed to do. By the
time the Honda engineer left, he knew almost everything
about Atlantic's operations and cost structure.

That knowledge proved useful when the two companies started doing business together in 1988. Japanese
companies traditionally work backward when setting
prices for the components and services they buy. Instead
of following the American practice of calculating costs,
adding a profit margin, and setting the product's price,

Japanese executives start with the price of the product they believe the market can bear. Then they figure out the costs they can incur to make the desired profits on that item. That practice allows the executives to set target prices: the amounts they can afford to pay suppliers for components and services given the budget for the product. Accordingly, when Honda submitted the target prices for the first jobs it gave Atlantic, both firms knew the supplier would make a profit. It would be a small profit, though, because Honda expected Atlantic to increase its profit margin by cutting costs over time.

A little empathy breeds a great deal of mutual understanding. Atlantic signed on partly because it believed Honda was acting fairly by allowing it to make a profit on the first deals. Because of the Honda engineer's visit, the supplier also felt confident that, with Honda's assistance, it would be able to reduce its costs. Once Atlantic had displayed its ability to handle Honda's orders, the automaker recommended the company to its other suppliers. As a result, Atlantic's business rose steadily during the next five years. It's interesting to note that around the same time, Atlantic attained the coveted Spear 1 supplier status at GM. That designation, GM claimed, would surely lead to more business with the manufacturer and its suppliers. But soon thereafter, GM reduced its orders with Atlantic without explanation. The supplier didn't get more business from GM during the next two years, and the partnership implied by the Spear 1 status never came to fruition.

## Turn Supplier Rivalry into Opportunity

*"Chrysler was our best customer, and we would break our back for them. Now we feel we're just another supplier. [It*

*has] put us in a bucket with everyone else, and we feel like
any other vendor."*
  —Senior executive, supplier to Daimler-Chrysler,
    July 1999

For all the feel-good talk about developing manufacturer-
supplier partnerships, Western executives still believe
that the keiretsu system is, at its core, inefficient and
inflexible. They assume that in the keiretsu model, companies are locked into buying components from specific
suppliers, a practice that leads to additional costs and
technological compromises. We find that assumption to
be incorrect. Neither Toyota nor Honda depends on a single source for anything; both develop two to three suppliers for every component or raw material they buy. They
may not want ten sources, as an American business
would, but they encourage competition between vendors
right from the product development stage. For example,
Toyota asked several suppliers in North America to
design tires for each of its vehicle programs. It evaluated
the performance of the tires based on the suppliers' data
as well as Toyota's road tests and awarded contracts to
the best vendors. The selected suppliers received contracts for the life of a model, but if a supplier's performance slipped, Toyota would award the next contract to
a competitor. If the supplier's performance improved,
Toyota might give it a chance to win another program
and regain its market share.

There is a key difference between the way American
and Japanese companies fuel the rivalry between their
suppliers. U.S. manufacturers set vendors against each
other and then do business with the last supplier stand-
ing. Toyota and Honda also spark competition between
vendors—especially when there is none—but only with

the support of their existing suppliers. In 1988, when Toyota decided to make cars in Kentucky, it picked Johnson Controls to supply seats. Johnson Controls wanted to expand its nearby facility, but Toyota stipulated that it shouldn't, partly because an expansion would require a large investment and eat into the supplier's profits. Instead, the Japanese manufacturer challenged Johnson Controls to make more seats in an existing building. That seemed impossible at first, but with the help of Toyota's lean-manufacturing experts, the supplier restructured its shop floor, slashed inventories, and was able to make seats for Toyota in the existing space. That experience helped the American vendor understand that it wasn't enough to deliver seats just in time; it had to use a system that would continually reduce its costs and improve quality. Such an approach would better align Johnson Controls' operating philosophy with Toyota's.

The relationship between manufacturer and supplier didn't end there. Six years later, when Toyota wanted to develop another source of seats, it refused to turn to another American manufacturer. Instead, it asked Johnson Controls if it was interested in entering into a joint venture with Toyota's biggest seat supplier in Japan, Araco, which was planning to enter the U.S. market. In 1987, Johnson Controls and Araco set up an American joint venture, Trim Masters, in which each held 40% of the equity and Toyota held 20%. Johnson Controls created a firewall so that Trim Masters would become a competitor in every sense of the word. A decade later, Trim Masters has become Johnson Controls' main rival for Toyota's seats business. In 2003, while Trim Masters had a 32% share of the business, Johnson Controls had a 56% share. Because of its investment in the joint venture, Johnson Controls has benefited from Trim Masters' success. Toyota turned a need to create competition between suppliers into an opportunity to cement its relationship with an existing vendor.

## Supervise Your Suppliers

*"[The Big Three] are hall monitors: I have to get from this door to that door, and they ask for my pass. You do everything you can to meet their objectives, but they keep putting barriers in the way."*
—Engineering director, Big Three supplier, April 2001

Vendors we talk to in Europe, the United States, and Mexico assume that Japanese-style partnerships are relationships between equals. They misconstrue win-win deals to mean that Toyota and Honda trust their suppliers enough to let them do their own thing. But in fact, the two Japanese automakers don't take a hands-off approach; they believe suppliers' roles are too vital for that. They use elaborate systems to measure the way their suppliers work, to set targets for them, and to monitor their performance at all times. Controls are the flip side of the trust that Toyota and Honda have in their suppliers.

Honda, for instance, uses a report card to monitor its core suppliers, some of which may be even second- or third-tier vendors. Unlike most *Fortune* 1,000 companies, which send reports to suppliers annually or biannually, Honda sends reports to its suppliers' top management every month. A typical report has six sections: quality, delivery, quantity delivered, performance history, incident report, and comments. The incident report section has a subcategory for quality and another for delivery. Honda uses the comments section to communicate how the supplier is doing. We've seen comments like "Keep up the good work" and "Please continue the effort; it is greatly appreciated." Honda also uses this section to highlight problems. For instance, Honda will write, "Label errors recorded on [part description and number]. Countermeasures presented weren't adequate."

Honda expects its core suppliers to meet all their targets on metrics like quality and delivery. If a vendor misses a target, the company reacts immediately. In early 1998, a tier-one supplier didn't meet an on-time-delivery target. Within hours of missing its deadline, the vendor came under intense scrutiny from Honda. It had to explain to the manufacturer how it would try to find the causes, how long that might take, and the possible measures it would employ to rectify the situation. Until it did that, the supplier had to promise to add extra shifts at its own cost to expedite order delivery. Both Toyota and Honda teach suppliers to take every problem seriously and to use problem-solving methodologies that uncover root causes. If suppliers aren't able to identify the causes, the manufacturers immediately send teams to help them. The manufacturers' engineers will facilitate the troubleshooting process, but the suppliers' engineers must execute the changes.

In contrast with most American companies, Toyota and Honda expect their suppliers' senior managers to get involved whenever issues arise. That expectation often causes problems. For example, in 1997, when a North American supplier ran into a design-related quality issue, the vice president of the Toyota Technical Center immediately invited his counterpart for a visit to discuss the matter. When the executive arrived, it became clear that he didn't understand the problem or its causes. "I don't get into that kind of detail," he stated. He was apologetic about the problem, however, and firmly assured his counterpart that he would take care of it. But that level of involvement wasn't enough for Toyota's managers. The Technical Center vice president asked the American executive to go and see for himself what the glitches were and return to discuss solutions when he understood the issues. Around the same time, Toyota found a quality problem with wire harnesses that Yazaki Corporation had supplied. The vendor's president flew to the Georgetown, Kentucky, plant and spent time on the shop floor observing how Toyota's workers assembled the harnesses. Only after the executive personally understood the situation did Yazaki formally present to Toyota the countermeasures it had already taken to fix the problem.

## Develop Compatible Technical Capabilities

*"[The term] 'supplier development' gives the impression that suppliers need to be developed. The reality is that we suppliers generally develop [the American automobile manufacturers'] people. They come in and tell us with an iron hand how to run our business, and we then have to train them about what we do!"*

—Managing director, supplier to one of the Big Three, August 1999

The notion of sourcing components from low-wage countries in Asia fascinates Western companies. Many U.S. automakers and their suppliers have set multibillion-dollar targets for purchasing components from China as if that would be an accomplishment in itself. That raises the question: Why haven't Toyota and

Honda switched to Chinese and Indian suppliers, too? According to our research, neither company sources very much from those countries primarily because suppliers there offer them only wage savings. That isn't enough for Toyota and Honda, which believe that suppliers' innovation capabilities are more important than their wage costs.

Toyota and Honda have invested heavily in improving the ability of their first-tier vendors to develop products. While their longtime suppliers like Denso, Aisin, and Araco can design components for the carmakers independently, North American vendors still don't know the manufacturers well enough to do so. For example, tires are critical to a vehicle's comfort, safety, handling, and noise level, but American vendors complain that Toyota and Honda give them vague specifications for new tires. Honda doesn't spell out the level of resistance it expects from a tire; it will only say that the tire has to have the right "feel"—a characteristic that is hard to quantify— and that it will be adjusted as the vehicle is designed. Toyota's engineers have developed a special vocabulary to describe the effect of tires on passengers. For instance, they use *gotsu gotsu* to refer to the low-frequency, high-impact motions tires transmit to passengers' lower backs and *buru buru* to describe the high-frequency, low-impact vibrations they feel in their belly. Toyota's engineers expect suppliers to understand what they are talking about and to identify solutions to problems the engineers describe. Until vendors learn to understand the terminology that Toyota and Honda use and are able to translate those vague requirements into design solutions, they can't develop new products for them.

That's why both companies have created guest engineer programs. Toyota and Honda ask first-tier suppliers to send several of their design engineers to the manufacturers' offices, where they work alongside the parent companies' engineers for two to three years. Eventually, the suppliers' engineers will understand the development process and come up with design ideas for Toyota and Honda. Meanwhile, the manufacturers have helped vendors by setting up learning links, forged by moving workers or launching transnational product development projects. For instance, since Toyota works with Denso in Japan, technology and knowledge transfers take place from Toyota's Japan operations to the Toyota Technical Center in Michigan and from Denso in Japan to Denso in Southfield, Michigan. Then the Toyota Technical Center and Denso work together to develop components for the U.S. market.

Toyota and Honda have also created checklists with hundreds of measurable characteristics for each component. American suppliers often don't have the data the Japanese companies demand because other manufacturers don't ask for them. Toyota and Honda start the product development process with their suppliers on-site by teaching them how to collect data. For example, Toyota expects precise data on the tolerances that the supplier's equipment can hold so it can design the product appropriately. One of its American suppliers didn't have that information for a component because it hadn't measured those parameters for decades. When Toyota discovered that, it helped the supplier set up a data collection system before the two companies figured out ways to improve the process. Clearly, as suppliers develop the capabilities to meet the Japanese manufacturers' requirements for data and design, they become more valuable to them than low-cost vendors without those capabilities could be.

## Share Information Intensively but Selectively

*"There's a danger in training [Chrysler's engineers]. Our people are very open, and they will tell our customers everything. They don't know that Chrysler's engineers later use that against us: 'So-and-so said you can do that in a week' [and that sort of thing]."*
   —Director of engineering, Chrysler supplier,
      August 1999

When Chrysler tried to build an American keiretsu in the early 1990s (see Jeffrey H. Dyer, "How Chrysler Created an American Keiretsu," HBR July–August 1996), it shared reams of data and held numerous meetings with suppliers. Chrysler's philosophy seemed to be, "If we inundate vendors with information and keep talking to them intensely, they will feel like partners." Toyota and Honda, however, believe in communicating and sharing information with suppliers selectively and in a structured fashion. Meetings have clear agendas and specific times and places, and there are rigid formats for information sharing with each supplier. The two Japanese companies know that sharing a lot of information with everyone ensures that no one will have the right information when it's needed.

Toyota and Honda share information carefully when they're developing new products with their suppliers. Toyota, for instance, divides components into two categories: those that vendors can design by themselves and those that must be developed at Toyota. The first category includes floor consoles, sunroofs, mirrors, locks, and other small components. Suppliers can design those components without much interaction with Toyota's engineers because the parts work relatively independent of the rest of the vehicle. The second category includes parts that interface with the sheet metal and trim of the body. Toyota must design these components more collaboratively with suppliers. It insists that suppliers develop the parts on Toyota's premises in close consultation with the manufacturer's engineers. At the Toyota Technical Center, the "design in" room houses suppliers who work in the same room on the same project. They design components into new vehicles using Toyota's CAD systems. Suppliers have to work at the Technical Center because Toyota gives them a lot of proprietary information, and they need to work hand in hand with Toyota engineers, especially during the early phases of a project.

The same principle—that inundating people with data diminishes focus while targeted information leads to results—extends to strategy. Honda uses only one top management meeting, or *jikon*, to share plans with each supplier. The meetings involve a Honda team—usually two vice presidents of supplier management and several assistant vice presidents—and a supplier team. The jikon happen within three months of the end of the fiscal year, which is when most suppliers make investment decisions and other strategic plans. Only core suppliers participate in the meetings, which take place at the regional and global levels. Honda invites one supplier from each region to the global jikon in Tokyo every year; it held one-on-one meetings with 35 North American suppliers in 2003. The discussions don't extend to operational matters but instead cover only top-level strategic issues. Honda tells the suppliers what kinds of products it intends to introduce and what types of markets it plans to cultivate in the coming years. The company then discusses the supplier's strategic direction in terms of technology, globalization, major investments (such as capital goods and plant expansion), and ideas about new products. The meetings also cover improvements that will be necessary in the quality, cost, and delivery of the vendor's products.

## Conduct Joint Improvement Activities

*"We're a showcase supplier for Toyota. Toyota improves its systems and shows how [implementing those changes will] improve [your production system, too]. We had discussions with [one of the Big Three's] so-called continuous improvement experts from Purchasing. He wanted to see what we were doing but didn't have much to add."*
    —Sales director, Big Three supplier, July 1999

Many American suppliers celebrated when they first received business from Toyota or Honda. They knew that in addition to new business, they would get opportunities to learn, to improve, and to enhance their reputations with other customers. Because Toyota and Honda are models of lean management, they bring about all-around improvements in their suppliers.

Honda, for example, has stationed a number of engineers in the United States, and they lead *kaizen* (continuous improvement) events at suppliers' facilities. While other automakers devote one day to a week to developing suppliers, Honda commits 13 weeks to its development program, which entails the creation of a model production line in the supplier's factory. Honda's engineers believe that the company's goals extend beyond technical consulting; the aim is to open communication channels and create relationships. That's why Honda's engineers stay in touch with suppliers long after returning to their own plants. That dedication to follow-through pays off: Honda's Best Practices program has increased suppliers' productivity by about 50%, improved quality by 30%, and reduced costs by 7%. That isn't entirely altruistic; suppliers have to share 50% of the cost savings with Honda. The reduced costs also become the baseline for new contracts that suppliers sign with Honda. However, the suppliers benefit, too, because they can apply what they have learned to their other product lines for Honda and its competitors and keep all those cost savings.

Similarly, Toyota teaches suppliers its famed Toyota Production System. The company has also set up *jishuken,* or study group teams, as a way to help the manufacturer and its suppliers learn together how to improve operations. Executives and engineers who work for Toyota and its suppliers meet under the direction of a Toyota sensei and go from plant to plant improving suppliers' processes. These activities, which are orchestrated in some cases by the Bluegrass Automotive Manufacturers Association (BAMA), Toyota's North American supplier group, give suppliers' managers hands-on experience with the Toyota Production System in different types of environments. The activities also create bonds among Toyota's suppliers because representatives of the vendors get together all through the year and share practices, information, and concerns.

In addition, BAMA provides support to suppliers that choose to help themselves. For example, in 2000, when Tenneco's Smithville, Tennessee, exhaust-systems plant decided to initiate a lean-manufacturing transformation, it turned to BAMA for help. Through the association, Tenneco's managers identified and visited some of the best lean suppliers in the United States. That experience helped them develop a vision. The managers then identified a lean-manufacturing expert within the company and went through a one-year transformation that included changing the plant layout. By 2002, the Tenneco plant had reduced head count by 39%, improved direct labor efficiency by 92%, eliminated $5 million of inventory, reduced defects in materials from 638 to 44 parts per million, and won a Toyota award for quality and delivery performance. Tenneco was a great student, but it also had a good mentor in BAMA.

THE FIRST STEP TOYOTA AND HONDA took to create lean enterprises was to develop suppliers to fill their North American needs. Once the foundation was in place, they moved on to the task of connecting suppliers into extended lean enterprises. This is still a work in progress. By establishing the six levels of the supplier-partnering hierarchy, Toyota and Honda have created a base on which their suppliers can continuously learn and get better. Many Toyota and Honda programs that appear to be short-term cost-cutting moves are actually experiments in learning. For example, Toyota thinks of its CCC21 initiative not as a price reduction program but as a way of creating a challenging environment that motivates its suppliers to improve. It's well aware that to achieve a 30% reduction in costs, vendors will have to question every operating assumption.

To be successful, an extended lean enterprise must have leadership from the manufacturer, partnerships between the manufacturer and suppliers, a culture of continuous improvement, and joint learning among the companies in the supplier network. That's what Toyota and Honda are ultimately trying to achieve through their remade-in-America keiretsu.

Originally published in December 2004
Reprint R0412G

# Rapid-Fire Fulfillment

KASRA FERDOWS, MICHAEL A. LEWIS, AND
JOSE A.D. MACHUCA

## Executive Summary

WOULD YOU SEND A HALF-EMPTY TRUCK across
Europe or pay to airfreight coats to Japan twice a week?
Would you move unsold items out of your shop after only
two weeks? Would you run your factories just during the
day shift? Is this any way to run an efficient supply chain?

For Spanish clothier Zara it is. Not that any one of
these tactics is especially effective in itself. Rather, they
stem from a holistic approach to supply chain management that optimizes the entire chain instead of focusing
on individual parts. In the process, Zara defies most of
the current conventional wisdom about how supply
chains should be run.

Unlike so many of its peers, which rush to outsource,
Zara keeps almost half of its production in-house. Far
from pushing its factories to maximize output, the company focuses capital on building extra capacity. Rather

than chase economies of scale, Zara manufactures and distributes products in small batches. Instead of outside partners, the company manages all design, warehousing, distribution, and logistics functions itself.

The result is a superresponsive supply chain exquisitely tailored to Zara's business model. Zara can design, produce, and deliver a new garment to its 600-plus stores worldwide in a mere 15 days. So in Zara's shops, customers can always find new products—but in limited supply. Customers think, "This green shirt fits me, and there is one on the rack. If I don't buy it now, I'll lose my chance." That urgency translates into high profit margins and steady 20% yearly growth in a tough economic climate.

Some of Zara's specific practices may be directly applicable only in industries where product life cycles are very short. But Zara's simple philosophy of reaping bottom-line profits through end-to-end control of the supply chain can be applied to any industry.

---

W HEN A GERMAN WHOLESALER suddenly canceled a big lingerie order in 1975, Amancio Ortega thought his fledgling clothing company might go bankrupt. All his capital was tied up in the order. There were no other buyers. In desperation, he opened a shop near his factory in La Coruña, in the far northwest corner of Spain, and sold the goods himself. He called the shop Zara.

Today, over 650 Zara stores in some 50 countries attract well-heeled customers in luxury shopping districts around the world, and Senor Ortega is arguably the richest man in Spain. The clothing company he founded, called Inditex, has been growing ever since he opened that first Zara shop. From 1991 to 2003, Inditex's sales—70% of which spring from Zara—grew more than 12-fold from €367 million to €4.6 billion, and net profits ballooned 14-fold from €31 million to €447 million. In May 2001, a particularly tough period for initial public offerings, Inditex sold 25% of its shares to the public for €2.3 billion. While many of its competitors have exhibited poor financial results over the last three years, Zara's sales and net income have continued to grow at an annual rate of over 20%.

The lesson Ortega learned from his early scare was this: To be successful, "you need to have five fingers touching the factory and five touching the customer." Translation: Control what happens to your product until the customer buys it. In adhering to this philosophy, Zara has developed a superresponsive supply chain. The company can design, produce, and deliver a new garment and put it on display in its stores worldwide in a mere 15 days. Such a pace is unheard-of in the fashion business, where designers typically spend months planning for the next season. Because Zara can offer a large variety of the latest designs quickly and in limited quantities, it collects 85% of the full ticket price on its retail clothing, while the industry average is 60% to 70%. As a result, it achieves a higher net margin on sales than its competitors; in 2001, for example, when Inditex's net margin was 10.5%, Benetton's was only 7%, H&M's was 9.5%, and Gap's was near zero.

Zara defies most of the current conventional wisdom about how supply chains should be run. In fact, some of Zara's practices may seem questionable, if not downright crazy, when taken individually. Unlike so many of its peers in retail clothing that rush to outsource, Zara keeps almost half of its production in-house. Far from pushing its factories to maximize their output, the company intentionally leaves extra capacity. Rather than chase economies of scale, Zara manufactures and distributes products in small batches. Instead of relying on outside partners, the company manages all design, warehousing, distribution, and logistics functions itself. Even many of its day-to-day operational procedures differ from the norm. It holds its retail stores to a rigid timetable for placing orders and receiving stock. It puts price tags on items before they're shipped, rather than at each store. It leaves large areas empty in its expensive retail shops. And it tolerates, even encourages, occasional stock-outs.

During the last three years, we've tried to discover just how Zara designs and manages its rapid-fire supply chain. We conducted a series of interviews with senior managers at Inditex and examined company documents and a wide range of other sources. We were particularly curious to see if Zara had discovered any groundbreaking innovations. We didn't find any. Instead, we found a self-reinforcing system built on three principles:

- **Close the communication loop.** Zara's supply chain is organized to transfer both hard data and anecdotal information quickly and easily from shoppers to designers and production staff. It's also set up to track materials and products in real time every step of the way, including inventory on display in the stores. The goal is to close the information loop between the end users and the upstream operations of design, procurement, production, and distribution as quickly and directly as possible.

- **Stick to a rhythm across the entire chain.** At Zara, rapid timing and synchronicity are paramount. To this end, the company indulges in an approach that can best be characterized as "penny foolish, pound wise." It spends money on anything that helps to increase and enforce the speed and responsiveness of the chain as a whole.

• **Leverage your capital assets to increase supply chain flexibility.** Zara has made major capital investments in production and distribution facilities and uses them to increase the supply chain's responsiveness to new and fluctuating demands. It produces complicated products in-house and outsources the simple ones.

It took Zara many years to develop its highly responsive system, but your company need not spend decades bringing its supply chain up to speed. Instead, you can borrow a page from Zara's playbook. Some of Zara's practices may be directly applicable only in high-tech or other industries where product life cycles are very short. But Ortega's simple philosophy of reaping profits through end-to-end control of the supply chain applies to any industry—from paper to aluminum products to medical instruments. Zara shows managers not only how to adjust to quixotic consumer demands but also how to resist management fads and ever-shifting industry practices.

## Close the Loop

In Zara stores, customers can always find new products—but they're in limited supply. There is a sense of tantalizing exclusivity, since only a few items are on display even though stores are spacious (the average size is around 1,000 square meters). A customer thinks, "This green shirt fits me, and there is one on the rack. If I don't buy it now, I'll lose my chance."

Such a retail concept depends on the regular creation and rapid replenishment of small batches of new goods. Zara's designers create approximately 40,000 new designs annually, from which 10,000 are selected for production. Some of them resemble the latest couture creations. But Zara often beats the high-fashion houses to the market and offers almost the same products, made with less expensive fabric, at much lower prices. Since most garments come in five to six colors and five to seven sizes, Zara's system has to deal with something in the realm of 300,000 new stock-keeping units (SKUs), on average, every year.

This "fast fashion" system depends on a constant exchange of information throughout every part of Zara's supply chain—from customers to store managers, from store managers to market specialists and designers, from designers to production staff, from buyers to subcontractors, from warehouse managers to distributors, and so on. Most companies insert layers of bureaucracy that can bog down communication between departments. But Zara's organization, operational procedures, performance measures, and even its office layouts are all designed to make information transfer easy.

Zara's single, centralized design and production center is attached to Inditex headquarters in La Coruña. It consists of three spacious halls—one for women's clothing lines, one for men's, and one for children's. Unlike most companies, which try to excise redundant labor to cut costs, Zara makes a point of running three parallel, but operationally distinct, product families. Accordingly, separate design, sales, and procurement and production-planning staffs are dedicated to each clothing line. A store may receive three different calls from La Coruña in one week from a market specialist in each channel; a factory making shirts may deal simultaneously with two Zara managers, one for men's shirts and another for children's shirts. Though it's more expensive to operate three channels, the information flow for each channel is fast, direct, and unencumbered by problems in other channels—making the overall supply chain more responsive.

In each hall, floor to ceiling windows overlooking the Spanish countryside reinforce a sense of cheery informality and openness. Unlike companies that sequester their design staffs, Zara's cadre of 200 designers sits right in the midst of the production process. Split among the three lines, these mostly twenty-something designers—hired because of their enthusiasm and talent, no prima donnas allowed—work next to the market specialists and procurement and production planners. Large circular tables play host to impromptu meetings. Racks of the latest fashion magazines and catalogs fill the walls. A small prototype shop has been set up in the corner of each hall, which encourages everyone to comment on new garments as they evolve.

The physical and organizational proximity of the three groups increases both the speed and the quality of the design process. Designers can quickly and informally check initial sketches with colleagues. Market specialists, who are in constant touch with store managers (and many of whom have been store managers themselves), provide quick feedback about the look of the new designs (style, color, fabric, and so on) and suggest possible market price points. Procurement and production planners make preliminary, but crucial, estimates of manufacturing costs and available capacity. The cross-functional teams can examine prototypes in the hall, choose a design, and commit resources for its production and introduction in a few hours, if necessary.

Zara is careful about the way it deploys the latest information technology tools to facilitate these informal exchanges. Customized handheld computers support the connection between the retail stores and La Coruña. These PDAs augment regular (often weekly) phone conversations between the store managers and the market specialists assigned to them. Through the PDAs and telephone conversations, stores transmit all kinds of information to La Coruña—such hard data as orders and sales trends and such soft data as customer reactions and the "buzz" around a new style. While any company can use PDAs to communicate, Zara's flat organization ensures that important conversations don't fall through the bureaucratic cracks.

Once the team selects a prototype for production, the designers refine colors and textures on a computer-aided design system. If the item is to be made in one of Zara's factories, they transmit the specs directly to the relevant cutting machines and other systems in that factory. Bar codes track the cut pieces as they are converted into garments through the various steps involved in production (including sewing operations usually done by subcontractors), distribution, and delivery to the stores, where the communication cycle began.

The constant flow of updated data mitigates the so-called bullwhip effect—the tendency of supply chains (and all open-loop information systems) to amplify small disturbances. A small change in retail orders, for example, can result in wide fluctuations in factory orders after it's transmitted through wholesalers and distributors. In an industry that traditionally allows retailers to change a maximum of 20% of their orders once the season has started, Zara lets them adjust 40% to 50%. In this way,

Zara avoids costly overproduction and the subsequent sales and discounting prevalent in the industry.

The relentless introduction of new products in small quantities, ironically, reduces the usual costs associated with running out of any particular item. Indeed, Zara makes a virtue of stock-outs. Empty racks don't drive customers to other stores because shoppers always have new things to choose from. Being out of stock in one item helps sell another, since people are often happy to snatch what they can. In fact, Zara has an informal policy of moving unsold items after two or three weeks. This can be an expensive practice for a typical store, but since Zara stores receive small shipments and carry little inventory, the risks are small; unsold items account for less than 10% of stock, compared with the industry average of 17% to 20%. Furthermore, new merchandise displayed in limited quantities and the short window of opportunity for purchasing items motivate people to visit Zara's shops more frequently than they might other stores. Consumers in central London, for example, visit the average store four times annually, but Zara's customers visit its shops an average of 17 times a year. The high traffic in the stores circumvents the need for advertising: Zara devotes just 0.3% of its sales on ads, far less than the 3% to 4% its rivals spend.

## Stick to a Rhythm

Zara relinquishes control over very little in its supply chain—much less than its competitors. It designs and distributes all its products, outsources a smaller portion of its manufacturing than its peers, and owns nearly all its retail shops. Even Benetton, long recognized as a pioneer in tight supply chain management, does not extend its reach as far as Zara does. Most of Benetton's stores are franchises, and that gives it less sway over retail inventories and limits its direct access to the critical last step in the supply chain—the customers.

This level of control allows Zara to set the pace at which products and information flow. The entire chain moves to a fast but predictable rhythm that resembles Toyota's "*Takt* time" for assembly or the "inventory velocity" of Dell's procurement, production, and distribution system. By carefully timing the whole chain, Zara avoids the usual problem of rushing through one step and waiting to take the next.

The precise rhythm begins in the retail shops. Store managers in Spain and southern Europe place orders twice weekly, by 3:00 p.m. Wednesday and 6:00 p.m. Saturday, and the rest of the world places them by 3:00 p.m. Tuesday and 6:00 p.m. Friday. These deadlines are strictly enforced: If a store in Barcelona misses the Wednesday deadline, it has to wait until Saturday.

Order fulfillment follows the same strict rhythm. A central warehouse in La Coruña prepares the shipments for every store, usually overnight. Once loaded onto a truck, the boxes and racks are either rushed to a nearby airport or routed directly to the European stores. All trucks and connecting airfreights run on established schedules—like a bus service—to match the retailers' twice-weekly orders. Shipments reach most European stores in 24 hours, U.S. stores in 48 hours, and Japanese shops in 72 hours, so store managers know exactly when the shipments will come in.

When the trucks arrive at the stores, the rapid rhythm continues. Because all the items have already been prepriced and tagged, and most are shipped hung up on racks, store managers can put them on display the moment they're delivered, without having to iron them. The need for control at this stage is minimized because the shipments are 98.9% accurate with less than 0.5% shrinkage. Finally, because regular customers know exactly when the new deliveries come, they visit the stores more frequently on those days.

This relentless and transparent rhythm aligns all the players in Zara's supply chain. It guides daily decisions by managers, whose job is to ensure that nothing hinders the responsiveness of the total system. It reinforces the production of garments in small batches, though larger batches would reduce costs. It validates the company policy of delivering two shipments every week, though less frequent shipment would reduce distribution costs. It justifies transporting products by air and truck, though ships and trains would lower transportation fees. And it provides a rationale for shipping some garments on hangers, though folding them into boxes would reduce the air and truck freight charges.

These counterintuitive practices pay off. Zara has shown that by maintaining a strict rhythm, it can carry less inventory (about 10% of sales, compared to 14% to 15% at Benetton, H&M, and Gap); maintain a higher profit margin on sales; and grow its revenues.

## Leverage Your Assets

In a volatile market where product life cycles are short, it's better to own fewer assets—thus goes the conventional wisdom shared by many senior managers, stock analysts, and management gurus. Zara subverts this logic. It produces roughly half of its products in its own factories. It buys 40% of its fabric from another Inditex firm, Comditel (accounting for almost 90% of Comditel's total sales), and it purchases its dyestuff from yet another Inditex company. So much vertical integration is clearly out of fashion in the industry; rivals like Gap and H&M, for example, own no production facilities. But Zara's managers reason that investment in capital assets can actually increase the organization's overall flexibility. Owning production assets gives Zara a level of control over schedules and capacities that, its senior managers argue, would be impossible to achieve if the company were entirely dependent on outside suppliers, especially ones located on the other side of the world.

The simpler products, like sweaters in classic colors, are outsourced to suppliers in Europe, North Africa, and Asia. But Zara reserves the manufacture of the more-complicated products, like women's suits in new seasonal colors, for its own factories (18 of which are in La Coruña, two in Barcelona, and one in Lithuania, with a few joint ventures in other countries). When Zara produces a garment in-house, it uses local subcontractors for simple and labor-intensive steps of the production process, like sewing. These are small workshops, each with only a few dozen employees, and Zara is their primary customer.

Zara can ramp up or down production of specific garments quickly and conveniently because it normally operates many of its factories for only a single shift. These highly automated factories can operate extra hours if need be to meet seasonal or unforeseen demands. Specialized by garment type, Zara's factories use sophisticated just-in-time systems, developed in cooperation with Toyota, that allow the company to customize its processes and exploit innovations. For example, like Benetton, Zara uses "postponement" to gain more speed and flexibility, purchasing more than 50% of its fabrics undyed so that it can react faster to midseason color changes.

All finished products pass through the five-story, 500,000-square-meter distribution center in La Coruña, which ships approximately 2.5 million items per week. There, the allocation of such resources as floor space, layout, and equipment follows the same logic that Zara applies to its factories. Storing and shipping many of its pieces on racks, for instance, requires extra warehouse space and elaborate material-handling equipment. Operating hours follow the weekly rhythm of the orders: In a normal week, this facility functions around the clock for four days but runs for only one or two shifts on the remaining three days. Ordinarily, 800 people fill the orders, each within eight hours. But during peak seasons, the company adds as many as 400 temporary staffers to maintain lead times.

Even though there's ample capacity in this distribution center during most of the year, Zara opened a new €100 million, 120,000-square-meter logistics center in Zaragoza, northeast of Madrid, in October 2003. Why is Zara so generous with capacity? Zara's senior managers follow a fundamental rule of queuing models, which holds that waiting time shoots up exponentially when capacity is tight and demand is variable (see the exhibit "For Fast Response, Have Extra Capacity on Hand"). By tolerating lower capacity utilization in its factories and distribution centers, Zara can react to peak or unexpected demands faster than its rivals.

Surprisingly, these practices don't burn up investment dollars. Thanks to the responsiveness of its factories and distribution centers, Zara has dramatically reduced its need for working capital. Because the company can sell its products just a few days after they're made, it can operate with negative working capital. The cash thus freed up helps offset the investment in extra capacity.

## Reinforcing Principles

None of the three principles outlined above—closing the communication loop, sticking to a rhythm, and leveraging your assets—is particularly new or radical. Each one alone could improve the responsiveness of any company's supply chain. But together, they create a powerful

---

### For Fast Response, Have Extra Capacity on Hand

*Zara's senior managers seem to comprehend intuitively the nonlinear relationship between capacity utilization, demand variability, and responsiveness. This relationship is well demonstrated by "queuing theory"—which explains that as capacity utilization begins to increase from low levels, waiting times increase gradually. But at some point, as the system uses more of the available capacity, waiting times accelerate rapidly. As demand becomes ever more variable, this acceleration starts at lower and lower levels of capacity utilization.*

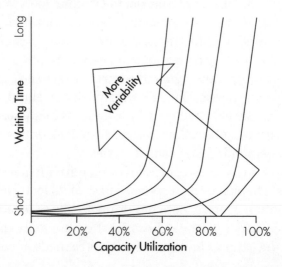

force because they reinforce one another. When a company is organized for direct, quick, and rich communications among those who manage its supply chain, it's easier to set a steady rhythm. Conversely, a strict schedule for moving information and goods through the supply chain makes it easier for operators at different steps to communicate with one another. And when the company focuses its own capital assets on responsiveness, it becomes simpler to maintain this rhythm. These principles, devotedly applied over many years, help to put together the jigsaw puzzle of Zara's practices.

Perhaps the deepest secret of Zara's success is its ability to sustain an environment that optimizes the entire supply chain rather than each step. Grasping the full implication of this approach is a big challenge. Few managers can imagine sending a half-empty truck across Europe, paying for airfreight twice a week to ship coats on hangers to Japan, or running factories for only one shift. But this is exactly why Zara's senior managers deserve credit. They have stayed the course and resisted setting performance measures that would make their operating managers focus on local efficiency at the expense of global responsiveness. They have hardwired into the organization the lesson Ortega learned almost 30 years ago: Touch the factories and customers with two hands. Do everything possible to let one hand help the other. And whatever you do, don't take your eyes off the product until it's sold.

**Originally published in November 2004**
**Reprint R0411G**

# Supply Chain Challenges:

## *Building Relationships*

A CONVERSATION WITH SCOTT BETH,
DAVID N. BURT, WILLIAM COPACINO,
CHRIS GOPAL, HAU L. LEE, ROBERT PORTER
LYNCH, AND SANDRA MORRIS

## Executive Summary

SUPPLY CHAIN MANAGEMENT IS all about software
and systems, right? Put in the best technology, sit back,
and watch as your processes run smoothly and the savings roll in? Apparently not.

When HBR convened a panel of leading thinkers in
the field of supply chain management, technology was
not top of mind. People and relationships were the dominant issues of the day. The opportunities and problems
created by globalization, for example, are requiring
companies to establish relationships with new types of
suppliers. The ever-present pressure for speed and cost
containment is making it even more important to break
down stubbornly high internal barriers and establish
more effective cross-functional relationships.

The costs of failure have never been higher. The
leading supply chain performers are applying new

technology, new innovations, and process thinking to far greater advantage than the laggards, reaping tremendous gains in all the variables that affect shareholder value: cost, customer service, asset productivity, and revenue generation. And the gap between the leaders and the losers is growing in almost every industry.

This roundtable gathered many of the leading thinkers and doers in the field of supply chain management, including practitioners Scott Beth of Intuit, Sandra Morris of Intel, and Chris Gopal of Unisys. David Burt of the University of San Diego and Stanford's Hau Lee bring the latest research from academia, Accenture's William Copacino and the Warren Company's Robert Porter Lynch offer the consultant's perspectives. Together, they take a wide-ranging view of such topics as developing talent, the role of the chief executive, and the latest technologies, exploring both the tactical and the strategic in the current state of supply chain management.

---

SUPPLY CHAIN MANAGEMENT IS all about software and systems, right? Get the best technology in place, then sit back and watch as your processes run smoothly and the savings roll in.

If that's true, then why did Jeff Bezos raid Wal-Mart's bench, paying top dollar to bring best-in-class logistics expertise to Amazon? Supply chains, it seems, are really about talent, not technology, especially as the marketplace grows ever more complex. But how to get people to work together?

It's not easy. When *Harvard Business Review* recently convened a panel of leading thinkers in the field of supply chain management, people and relationships were the dominant topics of the day. Creating effective alliances between companies, for instance, is complicated. Purchasing managers are rewarded for wringing the best possible price out of suppliers—a practice that's not conducive to nurturing long-standing partnerships. Internal relationships can be even more difficult to manage, according to one of our panelists. We've long known that functional silos hinder communication and efficiency, but many companies still struggle to tear down the walls.

Our panel, led by HBR senior editor Julia Kirby, explored these and such other obstacles and opportunities in supply chain management as developing talent, the role of the chief executive, and the latest technologies. The few companies that have cracked these nuts are gaining ground: The gap between the supply chain leaders and the average performers is large and growing. The following is an edited transcript of the panel's conversation.

**Julia Kirby:** I suspect that priorities in supply chain management have changed quite a bit in the last couple of years, for a variety of reasons. There's the economic downturn and the plunge into overcapacity. There's also terrorism and war. So I'd like to start by asking, What are the priorities today? Has your focus changed?

**Chris Gopal:** One area that's quite different from what it was a few years ago is, of course, security. The government has imposed, and is in the process of imposing, new regulations and requirements, particularly on companies doing business overseas, and a lot of them are not prepared for it. We've all heard about the stories of a ship being held up at a major port—at Long Beach, California, say—because it's got cargo that has set off alarm bells.

Another current priority is getting the tools we need to create an adaptive and responsive supply chain strategy—which is important because most supply chain strategies start down the road to being obsolete almost as soon as they're published. Creating an adaptive strategy starts with modeling the supply chain and doing scenario planning. That allows you to more effectively manage risk and cope with changes and uncertainty in the market, which in turn increases cash flow and customer retention. And then, once you execute your strategy, you need to be able to redo it based on patterns and trends derived from real-time information. Companies need tools for this kind of continual innovation—and there are none today.

**SANDRA MORRIS:** A big shift for Intel has been globalization. Our customer base is changing dramatically, not just in terms of where they live but also who they are and how they operate. There's huge potential in China, for example, and growing markets in Russia and India. That drives a different type of supply chain requirement. For example, the companies that are building and shipping PCs in emerging markets are small resellers, small distributors, not the typical multinational corporation we've worked with for decades. Their needs are different.

**WILLIAM COPACINO:** If you think back three to five years, the major issue for many companies was not to run out of parts. Today we have significant global overcapacity in most industries. So a key issue is managing the supply base—including sourcing, supplier integration, and in-bound parts management.

I also see a shift in focus from planning to execution. But I personally believe that there are huge opportunities on the planning side—in matching supply and demand. People are missing out because their attention, frankly, is so focused at the transactional level. We are seeing a shift back to basics—to MES [manufacturing execution systems] and WMS [warehouse management systems].

And we are beginning to see a growing interest in radio frequency identification—RFID—for several reasons. The cost of both chips and reader-writers is coming down rapidly, so the cost of solutions is becoming more competitive; the capabilities are expanding; and the need is growing in areas like theft protection and security.

**Scott Beth:** A big issue for us is misalignment of materials technologies and product life cycles. Say you're building instrumentation products that will last ten to 15 years using semiconductor components and other materials that may be available in the market for only 18 to 36 months before they're discontinued. This situation presents me with three alternatives: I have to buy and store a 13-year supply of components—that's a lot of extra inventory. Or I'm forced to mortgage the future by pulling engineers off new product development to reengineer products that still have a life in the marketplace. Or I have to find brokers or others who are willing to take the risk of holding onto unique and rapidly aging parts.

**Kirby: I'm struck that I'm not hearing you say, "Three years ago, the whole point of supply chain management was to increase speed, and now we're totally focused on cost reduction." Is that not happening?**

**Robert Porter Lynch:** To some extent, it is. The most disturbing trend that I've seen, with the meltdown of the stock market, has been cost cutting as a knee-jerk reaction. A chief financial officer will call the supply officer and say, "Cut costs 15%; we've got to get our stock price up." That knee-jerk reaction is having wholesale effects throughout the supply chain in very negative ways. You start to see cost cutting become a substitute for much more important competitive-advantage issues. A principle in business is that you cut costs to survive, but you innovate to prosper.

**BETH:** We're under incredible pressure to reduce material costs. But just as much on my mind is dealing with suppliers who aren't going to make it through this business downturn—many basic-component manufacturers are going out of business. When you're relying on a partner for unique technology, what do you do when they say they're locking their doors next week? How do you (a) find another source and (b) predict the health of suppliers so you can anticipate a shortfall before it happens?

**HAU L. LEE:** Cost is important, and so is speed. But I and my colleagues have been studying companies that have been hugely successful in the long run. And we've discovered that those companies are great not because they were focused on cost or flexibility or speed but because they have the ability to manage transitions—changing market conditions, evolving technology, different requirements as a product moves through its life cycle. The companies that can adapt are, I think, the ones that will be here for the long term.

These days, companies also need to be able to handle one more type of transition, which is crisis management. Successful companies have been able to grab market share and sales out of crises, which often requires them to work effectively across functional boundaries. I cite you the example of Zara, a Spanish apparel company. After September 11, which was, of course, a time of mourning, this company was able to get its designers, supply chain partners, and manufacturers together and in two weeks launch a new line of apparel featuring the color black. They got a tremendous sales lift as a result.

Companies like that have what I call the triple-A supply chain. They have agility, adaptability, and alignment. You need to align the interests of the functional groups and multiple partners so that you will be able to move forward in unison.

**KIRBY:** But we've known for 15 years that functional silos get in the way. Are the barriers starting to come down at all?

**LEE:** I still find many big corporations where each of the different functions do not know what the others are doing. A company might have promotion plans or a special trade deal in place, and the supply chain people are unaware of it. Or the supply chain manager plans how much inventory to put in place or how much capacity to invest in and doesn't share that with the sales and marketing people. And so you may find yourself in a situation where the sales and marketing people are giving special deals on a particular product when, in fact, you're running up to the capacity limit.

There are a lot of great examples of this disconnect. The most celebrated is Volvo, which made a lot of green cars in 1995 and wasn't able to sell them. So the sales and marketing people started to secretly offer heavy discounts, rebates, and special deals on green cars to their dealerships. The supply chain people didn't know that, and when they saw the green cars selling, they doubled their production plan for them for the next year. Volvo had a lot of green cars at the end of that year.

**MORRIS:** We've created a capability—five people, very senior program managers, who can look horizontally across functions. They bring together executives or senior managers and facilitate discussions about the tensions between product division goals, supply network goals, and customer goals. We have lots of people who are deep in their silos. They're also really smart. So getting them together on a fairly regular basis to deal with strategic topics in a facilitated session has been a breakthrough for us. It's probably been one of the best investments we've made.

**LYNCH:** Here's a data point. I'm the chairman emeritus of the Association of Alliance Professionals, and we did a survey last year of the critical issues concerning strategic alliance professionals throughout the world. We have 800 members. The number one concern these professionals had wasn't creating strategic alliances with other companies but creating alliances internally between the silos of their own company. For some reason, alliance professionals typically find it easier to create alliances with their major competitors than with other divisions in their own companies. We don't deal with our own internal integration. How do we integrate externally if we can't do it internally?

**GOPAL:** Way back in 1980, some studies were done as to why MRP [manufacturing resource planning] systems failed in implementation. One of the key reasons was this concept of silos, individual departments with their own metrics. To illustrate this, they came up with something called the Beer Game, in which you simulate a sudden change in demand and need to get your supply chain back into equilibrium. So now I'm sitting here in 2003 listening to exactly the same point and exactly the same comment about what makes these relationships successful. Has anything changed? Are we still dealing with the same problems in different forms?

COPACINO: Some companies are. But I think there's been a tremendous bifurcation of performance. In almost every industry, supply chain has become a much more important strategic and competitive variable. It affects all of the shareholder value levers—cost, customer service, asset productivity, and revenue generation. Yet we are seeing a growing gap in performance between the leading and the average companies. The best are getting better faster than the average companies across almost every industry. For instance from 1995 to 2001, Wal-Mart improved its inventory turns from 5.23 to 8.34. Its nearest competitor over that same time moved from 4.01 to just above five inventory turns, not even to the point where Wal-Mart started. And Dell operates with 64 to 100 inventory turns, more than two or three times most of its competitors. So, clearly, the performance gap is widening, and we see this happening in almost every industry segment.

The leading supply chain performers are applying new technology, new innovations, and new process thinking to great advantage. The average-performing companies and the laggards have a limited window of opportunity in which to catch up.

KIRBY: Robert mentioned that companies are having an easier time with external alliances than with internal ones. How are those external relationships evolving?

LYNCH: The best companies I see are beginning to triage the supply chain. In other words, they'll separate vendors that provide commodities from preferred suppliers that they have good relationships with from strategic suppliers that they create alliances with. They manage the supply base through those three different elements in very different ways, using different metrics, different processes, different people, and different mentalities.

**BETH:** Absolutely. I think that we have to determine, in Intel's case, where contract manufacturers fall along that spectrum. Speaking frankly, I think there's a love-hate relationship between OEMs and contract manufacturers. People don't trust the pricing they get, or there's a sort of bait-and-switch approach, where your prices start out low and then begin to creep up.

**KIRBY:** David, I see you nodding at this reference to trust. I know that issue is dear to your heart. What can you add?

**DAVID N. BURT:** Trust is the basis of agility, of flexibility. Yet it's an incredible challenge to establish trust and maybe even harder to maintain it. Underlying the challenge is the question of how to institutionalize trust between buyer and supplier. I've got colleagues who maintain that trust can only be established between individuals. But a few souls like Robert and myself say we've got to be able to institutionalize trust. We've got to make it work so that when the founders of the alliance depart, the alliance continues. We've been looking at this at USD for over ten years, and we don't have the answer yet.

But it's important. As the world gets more complicated, when I sell a product, I may be selling a solution that requires input from four or five companies. How do they get along with each other? If suppliers don't trust each other, the customer will be whipsawed. Also, trust enables you to make fast decisions, which lets you be more innovative and get rid of unproductive work. Trust is a competitive advantage.

**BETH:** You also lose out on efficiencies when trust isn't there. A lack of trust causes companies to duplicate activities between its own operations and its outsourced partners. Too often, we outsource an activity and then keep a lot of the management systems for that activity in place to verify that certain things are being done.

**LEE:** The way to build trust and establish a harmonious relationship is the third A of my triple-A: alignment—align the interests of the multiple parties so that they have some common values and goals.

A good example of alignment comes from Saturn. Saturn recognized that to provide good service in terms of the end customer's experience, it wouldn't be enough to be good at replenishing and supporting dealerships, which Saturn calls "retailers." The retailers also needed to have the right inventory. But Saturn understood that the retailers weren't necessarily good at inventory planning and forecasting. So the company asked retailers to let it take over the job of inventory management, and in return it offered to share their risk. If you're out of stock, Saturn will get the part to you from another retailer, overnight. Saturn even measures its own employees on how well the retailers serve their customers, the end users.

The result is that Saturn is always ranked among the top three in J.D. Power's Customer Satisfaction Index, even though it's competing with luxury cars. And Saturn retailers have a superior inventory performance—its average dealer inventory turn is about 7.5 a year versus the industry average of 2.5. Everybody wins when you have the right alignment.

**GOPAL:** I'd like to add a slightly different perspective. Trust is essential, of course. But before trust comes smart contracting. Trust is predicated on doing things jointly and in an aligned fashion over a period of time with no major surprises. However, to start with, the supply chain folks, who know the environment and the potential risks, need to get together with the people who develop the contracts so that managing risk—planning for alternative scenarios—can be embedded in the strategy and the contract. The next step is metrics. Trust can only be engendered by considering the risks and having joint metrics, with penalties and incentives. And over time, trust develops. I know that Scott does a lot of work in managing risk, working with different types of contracts with suppliers to generate some of that trust. Scott, do you have anything to tell us about this?

**BETH:** Our expectations for suppliers are changing. In the past, the contract manager would put a contract in front of me and point to a 3% price reduction over last year. The vector is right, and it's my only choice, so I'd sign off on it. But now what I expect is a series of choices that trade off price, inventory, and responsiveness. Those are the kinds of trade-offs that I need to be able to think about.

But on the issue of trust and penalties: We started off with a penalty approach, a clause that says if you don't provide us with a certain level of responsiveness, we'll charge you. And that began to erode trust. So instead we created an escrow account. If either party violates the agreement, money goes into the account, which is then used to reinvest in the relationship—new information systems, joint team education, and travel to get our people together more often. The level of trust went way up when we took this change in perspective.

**BURT:** These types of contracts and processes are critical. A company in our benchmark study—a large consumer products company—buys, for example, enzymes for its soap from a small company in Denmark. There are numerous intellectual property issues related to developing new chemical enzyme technologies, so naturally there are concerns about sharing ideas. The two companies worked out master agreements ahead of time so that they could develop and share new technologies without always having to go back to the lawyers and sign new legal agreements. They both placed a great deal of emphasis on ethics and had a clear understanding about the procedures, about what was expected from whom. The relationship was so good, and Natalie, the supply chain manager from the American company, fought so hard within her company on behalf of the supplier, that the Danish company named its latest enzyme Natalese for her.

So the relationship counts, but so does the process. They had a clear process governing how to work together, which allowed them to be constantly innovating and kept the relationship healthy.

**MORRIS:** I agree that good contracts are absolutely essential, but we've also seen that you can develop trust over time by increasing access to information and to experts within the company. That's particularly been the case with our e-business efforts, such as automatic replenishment of the factories. It starts with a pilot, with one trusted supplier, and it grows over time to become the standard way we do business.

We've watched the same kind of relationship grow among suppliers as we've created information repositories for fabrication equipment. When we develop a new technology, we work for years and years with both our customers and our suppliers before that technology is available, so products exist that use the technology when it's ready to ship. That sometimes involves a number of suppliers sharing information with each other as well as with Intel. The process, which began with three or four people who were willing to take that risk with us—to be fellow travelers—has now become a common way that we exchange information and develop new products.

**LYNCH:** Picking up on the idea of sharing with your partners in the value chain, there's an avenue of innovation that's just being completely missed, which is innovations that come from your suppliers. Dr. Burt did a study on this; I believe it was last year. And I think the average company said that 35% of its innovation came from the supply chain. Now, ask yourself, is that enough? Companies like Toyota are getting 60% of all their innovation out of the supply chain.

Here's a story. A client told me, "My largest customer is Johnson & Johnson. Every year, they come to me and they want a 5% to 15% price cut. I have piles of innovation to bring them. Every time I ask the supply chain manager, 'What about my innovations? Where do I take them?' He says, 'I'm not interested in that.' Why not? Because he's not rewarded for innovation. He's rewarded for cost cutting."

Another example: If you look at General Motors during the 1990s, warranty costs were higher than profits. Why were warranty costs so high? A lot of it is because GM wasn't looking to the supply chain for innovation. Chrysler, meanwhile, took massive amounts of market share because it was taking innovation through the supply chain. So, the question is, Do we prize it? Do we even measure it? Do we recognize the impact of supplier innovation on our competitive advantage? On customer satisfaction?

**GOPAL:** I'd like to go a level below all of that and say the companies I've seen that innovate best in the supply chain seem to be those that actually have the excellent people focused on the supply chain. I think it's a people issue, an issue of senior management focus and will. Michael Dell and his senior executives used to attend demand/supply-matching meetings. Dell executives are measured on joint metrics—they are (or at least they used to be) all measured on the same things—and that drives their focus on the supply chain as a competitive weapon.

Somebody once asked me about best practices. Well, knowledge is free. Everything that Dell, Wal-Mart, and 7-Eleven do is available somewhere on the Internet. Yet how many people can actually execute on it? The key is putting the system together right and making sure it works—managing risks and planning for contingencies through scenario planning, then executing and changing the strategy based on real-time trends.

Somebody also asked me about worst practices. I think the absolute worst practice is equating technology with the supply chain—the idea that "I buy a technology, so I've got a great supply chain." Nonsense. Innovation comes down to the people, the tools, and what value senior management places on it. I'd like to ask Hau, How many students at Stanford go into management of the supply chain?

**KIRBY: I think a lot of people woke up to the talent component of supply chain management when Amazon quite visibly and famously raided Wal-Mart's supply chain management talent. That was a surprise to a lot of people who thought supply chain was mainly about technology and how much money you spent on distribution center design and the like. But is it really about talent, Hau?**

LEE: I agree that people—and in particular the leadership—are a very important part of supply chain management. Toshifumi Suzuki, the chairman of Seven-Eleven

Japan, spends a whole morning each week reviewing the previous week's supply chain performance. It shows his passion, and it shows his commitment and interest.

In terms of our students at Stanford, electives on supply chain used to be unpopular, but now we have to offer more sections. I know my colleagues at other schools are seeing the same thing. And it's because we have companies like Dell, Seven-Eleven Japan, and Zara that are hiring talented people and giving them opportunities for a great career path, showing them that supply chain is not about just managing within these four walls. And the difference is not in cost containment but in innovation and value creation.

**KIRBY: Scott, are you seeing that? Is your talent pool rising?**

**BETH:** Yes. When I meet with a group of procurement professionals, I ask them about their backgrounds. In the past, I got primarily teachers, real estate agents, accountants, administrators, political scientists, sometimes a lawyer or two. Now I'm finding the population shifting toward supply chain professionals, people who are coming with that training.

**KIRBY: So talent is key. But what about technology? Is it not as fundamental as some people believe?**

**BURT:** There are two schools of thought. One is that by getting the right software we can get rid of people. It's that simple. The other is that IT and other technologies are enablers, and they can be tremendous assets when you have the right people in place. But if your CEO or CFO thinks that you're going to get rid of people because you bought whatever software, I'm not sure it's a place you want to work.

**MORRIS:** Some amazing information technology has arrived on the scene, RosettaNet being one in the PC supply chain. It's a story of incredible cooperation among competitors—400 companies got together to define business processes at a pretty tactical level. How do we treat an order? How do we treat a return? How do we treat an advance-shipping notice? What fields do we need so that we can have machine-to-machine communication, allowing a distributor to connect to 35 suppliers and not have to create point-to-point business processes and reconcile data on the back end on a daily basis?

Last year, we did about 10% of our transactions with customers using the RosettaNet standard. I don't think it will completely replace EDI, but we think over time it will become a standard way for us to connect, for certain types of transactions. It's more efficient, not because we think we can lower head count but because we can get people out of the day-to-day business of reconciling and touching purchase orders that should never be touched and get them to focus on higher-order service and strategies for the company.

**LEE:** Technology—hardware as well as software—is without question crucial in supply chain management. But technology can break the company as well as enable the company to be hugely successful. The distinction is in how people use their technology. Technology is an enabler. You can turn it into power and then receive C-level attention. It depends on the people.

**COPACINO:** One of the critical findings out of our research was exactly that: The masters—the leading companies—are extraordinarily good at selectively choosing what technologies to implement. Others—the average-performing companies and the laggards—are broader and less selective in deciding what technology solutions to implement. And the masters are very disciplined in their implementation, focusing on process design and effective program management and change management.

LYNCH: I would add that companies are much more cautious now about technology because there were so many implementation bungles that drove companies up the wall. They are now much more careful to make sure that an implementation is going to go according to plan and it's going to meet the company's needs. Whereas three or four years ago, so many companies were implementing technology willy-nilly because they thought it was a cure-all.

KIRBY: **What about RFID? Is it real? Is it overhyped? What's the ROI horizon?**

COPACINO: We have seen a significant pickup in interest and successful pilots over the last six months. As prices come down, with chip prices that are now approaching 20 cents and will over time go to five cents, RFID becomes very valuable from a productivity point of view. Price points are coming down on reading equipment, too.

We are actively working on probably nine or ten applications, particularly in areas where there's concern about theft. But, more fundamentally, we're also seeing broader efficiency and operational improvements over traditional processes, methods, and technologies.

GOPAL: The application is everywhere. Retail is one. Ford uses a real-time logistics system for visibility through triangulation. Container people use it for tracking. And I think, with Operation Safe Commerce, now it's going to be even more in demand. Adoption will go by industry.

Five cents is a good-enough price point for some heavy industrial manufacturing. One cent will be good enough for very low-margin consumables, maybe. It's a question of economics and end-to-end visibility.

**LEE:** I think RFID will evolve much as e-commerce has evolved. When e-commerce first came out, it just automated existing processes and work flows. You could send a purchase order by the Internet or pay an invoice or communicate through e-mail. You were substituting an existing technology for a new one, but you were doing the same thing.

That's not the biggest impact of e-commerce. As Sandra described, the biggest value comes when you can do things like collaborate with your suppliers, as Microsoft did when it used the Internet to collaborate on the design for the Xbox. And you can also use e-commerce to change a process. For example, e-commerce can allow manufacturers to ship products directly to consumers, bypassing multiple layers of distribution channels. It's the process changes that create the greater value.

RFID will follow the same kind of evolution. Now it's mostly tracking. Instead of physically counting how many items you have on the shelf, the technology can read it, and you know instantly. You want to find out when an item left the store? You know instantly. This is automating an existing process that you're currently doing manually. That's the first level but not the biggest impact. I think the biggest value will come from new applications that use the technology's intelligence. RFID can create a borderless supply chain when cargoes are equipped with tags showing the contents, so that customs clearance can be done almost automatically. RFID can also provide supply chain security when RFID tags are used to electronically seal containers and monitor movements of the containers, so that any tampering can be tracked.

KIRBY: I have one more question, which touches on a number of things we've talked about today—sharing information with customers and suppliers, developing alliances, innovating with suppliers. My question is, When do we stop talking about the supply chain and start talking about the value chain?

LYNCH: The problem with value chain is that most people haven't really started to think about it. It's not taught in the university; we don't have a value chain professor. It's like strategic alliances: It sort of grew organically. But in many industries, the leaders actually have shifted from supply chain to value chain, even if they haven't branded it that. Look at what Wal-Mart did to Kmart. That's a value chain story, not just supply chain. Some other companies are very good at managing the value chain as well. Southwest Airlines has it figured all the way out from the customer right back through the whole chain. Dell Computer is managing the chain from the customer all the way back through the supply networks. Another is Harley-Davidson. And Saturn, as Hau showed us.

I'm going to predict that within five years, we will have the battle of the value chains. And then it will shift to value networks after that.

BURT: Robert, I know it's always dangerous to disagree with you, but I'll put myself in jeopardy and point out that our recently approved master of science in supply chain management has a capstone course called Value Chain Management.

GOPAL: I look at value chains and supply chains almost synonymously, and I'm trying to figure out the difference. The word "value" is one that I fundamentally distrust,

having been burned by it in so many different environments. And I'm trying to figure out what you mean when
you talk about value chain versus supply chain. Are they
really different? I don't buy "new-name proliferation."

**COPACINO:** You get into semantics on this. I was asked
by the Council of Logistics Management to develop a
definition of supply chain and logistics. We had six
prominent people on the committee I formed, and we
could not agree on a single definition.

But I take the same perspective that Chris does. I
think that supply chain done right is a value chain. It's an
integrated supply and demand chain or an integrated
value chain. When you think about it that way, you use it
to drive revenues and innovation and create value—not
just to reduce cost. And that's where you start to get
strategic advantage.

---

## The panelists (Alphabetical order)

**Scott Beth** is the vice president of procurement at Intuit.
At the time of the roundtable, Beth was a senior director
of global sourcing for Agilent Technologies' electronic
products and solutions group.

**David N. Burt** is a professor of supply chain management and the director of the University of San Diego's
Institute of Supply Chain Management.

**William Copacino** is the group chief executive of
Accenture's Business Consulting capability group. He is
the author of several books on supply chain management, including *Supply Chain Management: The Basics
and Beyond* (St. Lucie Press, 1997).

**Chris Gopal** is the vice president of global supply chain management at Unisys. Previously he was the director of global supply chain consulting at Ernst & Young and a vice president at Dell Computer.

**Hau L. Lee** is the Thoma Professor of Operations, Information, and Technology at Stanford University, codirector of the Stanford Global Supply Chain Management Forum, and director of the Managing Your Supply Chain for Global Competitiveness Executive Program.

**Robert Porter Lynch** is the CEO of the Warren Company. He is the author of *Business Alliances Guide: The Hidden Competitive Weapon* (Wiley, 1993).

**Sandra Morris** is a vice president and the chief information officer of Intel, where she has been since 1985. Previously, she was at the David Sarnoff Research Center of RCA.

**Originally published in July 2003**
**Reprint R0307E**

# The Triple-A Supply Chain

HAU L. LEE

## Executive Summary

BUILDING A STRONG SUPPLY CHAIN is essential for business success. But when it comes to improving their supply chains, few companies take the right approach. Many businesses work to make their chains faster or more cost-effective, assuming that those steps are the keys to competitive advantage. To the contrary: Supply chains that focus on speed and costs tend to deteriorate over time.

The author has spent 15 years studying more than 60 companies to gain insight into this and other supply chain dilemmas. His conclusion: Only companies that build supply chains that are agile, adaptable, and aligned get ahead of their rivals. All three components are essential; without any one of them, supply chains break down.

Great companies create supply chains that respond to abrupt changes in markets. Agility is critical because in most industries, both demand and supply fluctuate rapidly and widely. Supply chains typically cope by playing speed against costs, but agile ones respond both quickly and cost-efficiently.

Great companies also adapt their supply networks when markets or strategies change. The best supply chains allow managers to identify structural shifts early by recording the latest data, filtering out noise, and tracking key patterns.

Finally, great companies align the interests of the partners in their supply chains with their own. That's important because every firm is concerned solely with its own interests. If its goals are out of alignment with those of other partners in the supply chain, performance will suffer.

When companies hear about the triple-A supply chain, they assume that building one will require increased technology and investment. But most firms already have the infrastructure in place to create one. A fresh attitude alone can go a long way toward making it happen.

---

DURING THE PAST DECADE AND A HALF, I've studied from the inside more than 60 leading companies that focused on building and rebuilding supply chains to deliver goods and services to consumers as quickly and inexpensively as possible. Those firms invested in state-of-the-art technologies, and when that proved to be inadequate, they hired top-notch talent to boost supply chain performance. Many companies also teamed up to streamline processes, lay down technical standards, and invest in infrastructure they could share. For instance, in the early 1990s, American apparel companies started a Quick Response initiative, grocery companies in Europe and the United States touted a program called Efficient Consumer Response, and the U.S. food service industry embarked on an Efficient Foodservice Response program.

All those companies and initiatives persistently aimed at greater speed and cost-effectiveness—the popular grails of supply chain management. Of course, companies' quests changed with the industrial cycle: When business was booming, executives concentrated on maximizing speed, and when the economy headed south, firms desperately tried to minimize supply costs.

As time went by, however, I observed one fundamental problem that most companies and experts seemed to ignore: Ceteris paribus, companies whose supply chains became more efficient and cost-effective didn't gain a sustainable advantage over their rivals. In fact, the performance of those supply chains steadily deteriorated. For instance, despite the increased efficiency of many companies' supply chains, the percentage of products that were marked down in the United States rose from less than 10% in 1980 to more than 30% in 2000, and surveys show that consumer satisfaction with product availability fell sharply during the same period.

Evidently, it isn't by becoming more efficient that the supply chains of Wal-Mart, Dell, and Amazon have given those companies an edge over their competitors. According to my research, top-performing supply chains possess three very different qualities. First, great supply chains are agile. They react speedily to sudden changes in demand or supply. Second, they adapt over time as market structures and strategies evolve. Third, they align the interests of all the firms in the supply network so that companies optimize the chain's performance when they maximize their interests. Only supply chains that are agile, adaptable, and aligned provide companies with sustainable competitive advantage.

## The Perils of Efficiency

Why haven't efficient supply chains been able to deliver the goods? For several reasons. High-speed, low-cost supply chains are unable to respond to unexpected changes in demand or supply. Many companies have centralized manufacturing and distribution facilities to generate scale economies, and they deliver only container loads of products to customers to minimize transportation time, freight costs, and the number of deliveries. When demand for a particular brand, pack size, or assortment rises without warning, these organizations are unable to react even if they have the items in stock. According to two studies I helped conduct in the 1990s, the required merchandise was often already in factory stockyards, packed and ready to ship, but it couldn't be moved until each container was full. That "best" practice delayed shipments by a week or more, forcing stocked-out stores to turn away consumers. No wonder then that, according to another recent research report, when companies announce product promotions, stock outs rise to 15%, on average, even when executives have primed supply chains to handle demand fluctuations.

When manufacturers eventually deliver additional merchandise, it results in excess inventory because most distributors don't need a container load to satisfy the increased demand. To get rid of the stockpile, companies mark down those products sooner than they had planned to. That's partly why department stores sell as much as a third of their merchandise at discounted prices. Those markdowns not only reduce companies' profits but also erode brand equity and anger loyal customers who bought the items at full price in the recent past (sound familiar?).

Companies' obsession with speed and costs also causes supply chains to break down during the launch of new products. Some years ago, I studied a well-known consumer electronics firm that decided not to create a buffer stock before launching an innovative new product. It wanted to keep inventory costs low, particularly since it hadn't been able to generate an accurate demand forecast. When demand rose soon after the gizmo's launch and fell sharply thereafter, the company pressured vendors to boost production and then to slash output. When demand shot up again a few weeks later, executives enthusiastically told vendors to step up production once more. Five days later, supplies of the new product dried up as if someone had turned off a tap.

The shocked electronics giant discovered that vendors had been so busy ramping production up and down that they hadn't found time to fix bugs in both the components' manufacturing and the product's assembly processes. When the suppliers tried to boost output a second time, product defects rose to unacceptable levels, and some vendors, including the main assembler, had to shut down production lines for more than a week. By the time the suppliers could fix the glitches and restart production, the innovation was all but dead. If the electronics company had given suppliers a steady, higher-than-needed manufacturing schedule until both the line and demand had stabilized, it would have initially had higher inventory costs, but the product would still be around.

Efficient supply chains often become uncompetitive because they don't adapt to changes in the structures of markets. Consider Lucent's Electronic Switching Systems division, which set up a fast and cost-effective supply chain in the late 1980s by centralizing component procurement, assembly and testing, and order fulfillment in Oklahoma City. The supply chain worked brilliantly as long as most of the demand for digital switches emanated from the Americas and as long as Lucent's vendors were mostly in the United States. However, in the 1990s, when Asia became the world's fastest-growing market, Lucent's response times increased because it hadn't set up a plant in the Far East. Furthermore, the company couldn't customize switches or carry out modifications because of the amount of time and money it took the supply chain to do those things across continents.

Lucent's troubles deepened when vendors shifted manufacturing facilities from the United States to Asia to take advantage of the lower labor costs there. "We had to fly components from Asia to Oklahoma City and fly them back again to Asia as finished products. That was costly and time consuming," Lucent's then head of manufacturing told me. With tongue firmly in cheek, he added, "Neither components nor products earned frequent-flyer miles." When Lucent redesigned its supply chain in 1996 by setting up joint ventures in Taiwan and China to manufacture digital switches, it did manage to gain ground in Asia.

In this and many other cases, the conclusion would be the same: Supply chain efficiency is necessary, but it isn't enough to ensure that firms will do better than their rivals. Only those companies that build agile, adaptable, and aligned supply chains get ahead of the competition, as I pointed out earlier. In this article, I'll expand on each of those qualities and explain how companies can build them into supply chains without having to make trade-offs. In fact, I'll show that any two of these dimensions alone aren't enough. Only companies that build all three into supply chains become better faster than their rivals. I'll conclude by describing how Seven-Eleven Japan has become one of the world's most profitable retailers by building a truly "triple-A" supply chain. (See "Building the Triple-A Supply Chain" at the end of this article.)

## Fostering Agility

Great companies create supply chains that respond to sudden and unexpected changes in markets. Agility is critical, because in most industries, both demand and supply fluctuate more rapidly and widely than they used to. Most supply chains cope by playing speed against costs, but agile ones respond both quickly and cost-efficiently.

Most companies continue to focus on the speed and costs of their supply chains without realizing that they pay a big price for disregarding agility. (See "The Importance of Being Agile" at the end of this article.) In the 1990s, whenever Intel unveiled new microprocessors, Compaq took more time than its rivals to launch the next generation of PCs because of a long design cycle. The company lost mind share because it could never count early adopters, who create the buzz around high-tech products, among its consumers. Worse, it was unable to compete on price. Because its products stayed in the pipeline for a long time, the company had a large inventory of raw materials. That meant Compaq didn't reap much benefit when component prices fell, and it couldn't cut PC prices as much as its rivals were able to. When vendors announced changes in engineering specifications, Compaq incurred more reworking costs than other manufacturers because of its larger work-in-progress inventory. The lack of an agile supply chain caused Compaq to lose PC market share throughout the decade.

By contrast, smart companies use agile supply chains to differentiate themselves from rivals. For instance, H&M, Mango, and Zara have become Europe's most profitable apparel brands by building agility into every link of their supply chains. At one end of their product pipelines, the three companies have created agile design processes. As soon as designers spot possible trends, they create sketches and order fabrics. That gives them a head start over competitors because fabric suppliers require the longest lead times. However, the companies finalize designs and manufacture garments only after they get reliable data from stores. That allows them to make products that meet consumer tastes and reduces the number of items they must sell at a discount. At the other end of the pipeline, all three companies have superefficient distribution centers. They use state-of-the-art sorting and material-handling technologies to ensure that distribution doesn't become a bottleneck when they must respond to demand fluctuations. H&M, Mango, and Zara have all grown at more than 20% annually since 1990, and their double-digit net profit margins are the envy of the industry.

Agility has become more critical in the past few years because sudden shocks to supply chains have become frequent. The terrorist attack in New York in 2001, the dockworkers' strike in California in 2002, and the SARS epidemic in Asia in 2003, for instance, disrupted many companies' supply chains. While the threat from natural disasters, terrorism, wars, epidemics, and computer viruses has intensified in recent years, partly because supply lines now traverse the globe, my research shows that most supply chains are incapable of coping with emergencies. Only three years have passed since 9/11, but U.S. companies have all but forgotten the importance of drawing up contingency plans for times of crisis.

Without a doubt, agile supply chains recover quickly from sudden setbacks. In September 1999, an earthquake in Taiwan delayed shipments of computer components to the United States by weeks and, in some cases, by months. Most PC manufacturers, such as Compaq, Apple, and Gateway, couldn't deliver products to customers on time and incurred their wrath. One exception was Dell, which changed the prices of PC configurations overnight. That allowed the company to steer consumer demand away from hardware built with components that weren't available toward machines that didn't use those parts. Dell could do that because it got data on the earthquake damage early, sized up the extent of vendors' problems quickly, and implemented the plans it had drawn up to cope with such eventualities immediately. Not surprisingly, Dell gained market share in the earthquake's aftermath.

Nokia and Ericsson provided a study in contrasts when in March 2000, a Philips facility in Albuquerque, New Mexico, went up in flames. The plant made radio frequency (RF) chips, key components for mobile telephones, for both Scandinavian companies. When the fire damaged the plant, Nokia's managers quickly carried out design changes so that other companies could manufacture similar RF chips and contacted backup sources. Two suppliers, one in Japan and another in the United States, asked for just five days' lead time to respond to Nokia. Ericsson, meanwhile, had been weeding out backup suppliers because it wanted to trim costs. It didn't have a plan B in place and was unable to find new chip suppliers. Not only did Ericsson have to scale back production for months after the fire, but it also had to delay the launch of a major new product. The bottom line: Nokia stole market share from Ericsson because it had a more agile supply chain.

Companies can build agility into supply chains by adhering to six rules of thumb:

- Provide data on changes in supply and demand to partners continuously so they can respond quickly. For instance, Cisco recently created an e-hub, which connects suppliers and the company via the Internet. This allows all the firms to have the same demand and supply data at the same time, to spot changes in demand or supply problems immediately, and to respond in a concerted fashion. Ensuring that there are no information delays is the first step in creating an agile supply chain.

- Develop collaborative relationships with suppliers and customers so that companies work together to design or redesign processes, components, and products as well as to prepare backup plans. For instance, Taiwan Semiconductor Manufacturing Company (TSMC), the world's largest semiconductor foundry, gives suppliers and customers proprietary tools, data, and models so they can execute design and engineering changes quickly and accurately.

- Design products so that they share common parts and processes initially and differ substantially only by the end of the production process. I call this strategy "postponement." (See the January-February 1997 HBR article I coauthored with Edward Feitzinger, "Mass Customization at Hewlett-Packard: The Power of

Postponement.") This is often the best way to respond quickly to demand fluctuations because it allows firms to finish products only when they have accurate information on consumer preferences. Xilinx, the world's largest maker of programmable logic chips, has perfected the art of postponement. Customers can program the company's integrated circuits via the Internet for different applications after purchasing the basic product. Xilinx rarely runs into inventory problems as a result.

- Keep a small inventory of inexpensive, nonbulky components that are often the cause of bottlenecks. For example, apparel manufacturers H&M, Mango, and Zara maintain supplies of accessories such as decorative buttons, zippers, hooks, and snaps so that they can finish clothes even if supply chains break down.

- Build a dependable logistics system that can enable your company to regroup quickly in response to unexpected needs. Companies don't need to invest in logistics systems themselves to reap this benefit; they can strike alliances with third-party logistics providers.

- Put together a team that knows how to invoke backup plans. Of course, that's possible only if companies have trained managers and prepared contingency plans to tackle crises, as Dell and Nokia demonstrated.

## Adapting Your Supply Chain

Great companies don't stick to the same supply networks when markets or strategies change. Rather, such organizations keep adapting their supply chains so they can adjust to changing needs. Adaptation can be tough, but it's critical in developing a supply chain that delivers a sustainable advantage.

Most companies don't realize that in addition to unexpected changes in supply and demand, supply chains also face near-permanent changes in markets. Those structural shifts usually occur because of economic progress, political and social change, demographic trends, and technological advances. Unless companies adapt their supply chains, they won't stay competitive for very long. Lucent twice woke up late to industry shifts, first to the rise of the Asian market and later to the advantages of outsourced manufacturing. (See "Adaptation of the Fittest" at the end of this article.) Lucent recovered the first time, but the second time around, the company lost its leadership of the global telecommunications market because it didn't adapt quickly enough.

The best supply chains identify structural shifts, sometimes before they occur, by capturing the latest data, filtering out noise, and tracking key patterns. They then relocate facilities, change sources of supplies, and, if possible, outsource manufacturing. For instance, when Hewlett-Packard started making ink-jet printers in the 1980s, it set up both its R&D and manufacturing divisions in Vancouver, Washington. HP wanted the product development and production teams to work together because ink-jet technology was in its infancy, and the biggest printer market was in the United States. When demand grew in other parts of the world, HP set up manufacturing facilities in Spain and Singapore to cater to Europe and Asia. Although Vancouver remained the site where HP developed new printers, Singapore became the largest production facility because the company needed economies of scale to survive. By the mid-1990s, HP real-

ized that printer-manufacturing technologies had
matured and that it could outsource production to vendors completely. By doing so, HP was able to reduce
costs and remain the leader in a highly competitive
market.

Adaptation needn't be just a defensive tactic. Companies that adapt supply chains when they modify strategies often succeed in launching new products or breaking into new markets. Three years ago, when Microsoft
decided to enter the video game market, it chose to outsource hardware production to Singapore-based Flextronics. In early 2001, the vendor learned that the Xbox
had to be in stores before December because Microsoft
wanted to target Christmas shoppers. Flextronics reck-
oned that speed to market and technical support would
be crucial for ensuring the product's successful launch.
So it decided to make the Xbox at facilities in Mexico
and Hungary. The sites were relatively expensive, but
they boasted engineers who could help Microsoft make
design changes and modify engineering specs quickly.
Mexico and Hungary were also close to the Xbox's
biggest target markets, the United States and Europe.
Microsoft was able to launch the product in record time
and mounted a stiff challenge to market leader Sony's
PlayStation 2. Sony fought back by offering deep discounts on the product. Realizing that speed would not be
as critical for medium-term survival as costs would be,
Flextronics shifted the Xbox's supply chain to China. The
resulting cost savings allowed Microsoft to match Sony's
discounts and gave it a fighting chance. By 2003, the
Xbox had wrested a 20% share of the video game market
from PlayStation 2.

Smart companies tailor supply chains to the nature of
markets for products. They usually end up with more

than one supply chain, which can be expensive, but they also get the best manufacturing and distribution capabilities for each offering. For instance, Cisco caters to the demand for standard, high-volume networking products by commissioning contract manufacturers in low-cost countries such as China. For its wide variety of mid-value items, Cisco uses vendors in low-cost countries to build core products but customizes those products itself in major markets such as the United States and Europe. For highly customized, low-volume products, Cisco uses vendors close to main markets, such as Mexico for the United States and Eastern European countries for Europe. Despite the fact that it uses three different supply chains at the same time, the company is careful not to become less agile. Because it uses flexible designs and standardized processes, Cisco can switch the manufacture of products from one supply network to another when necessary.

Gap, too, uses a three-pronged strategy. It aims the Old Navy brand at cost-conscious consumers, the Gap line at trendy buyers, and the Banana Republic collection at consumers who want clothing of higher quality. Rather than using the same supply chain for all three brands, Gap set up Old Navy's manufacturing and sourcing in China to ensure cost efficiency, Gap's chain in Central America to guarantee speed and flexibility, and Banana Republic's supply network in Italy to maintain quality. The company consequently incurs higher overheads, lower scale economies in purchasing and manufacturing, and larger transportation costs than it would if it used just one supply chain. However, since its brands cater to different consumer segments, Gap uses different kinds of supply networks to maintain distinctive positions. The adaptation has worked. Many consumers don't realize that Gap owns all three brands, and the three chains serve as backups in case of emergency.

Sometimes it's difficult for companies to define the appropriate markets, especially when they are launching innovative new products. The trick is to remember that products embody different levels of technology. For instance, after records came cassettes and then CDs. Videotapes were followed by DVDs, and almost anything analog is now or will soon become digital. Also, every product is at a certain stage of its life cycle, whether it's at the infant, ramp-up, mature, or end-of-life stage. By mapping either or both of those characteristics to supply chain partners, manufacturing network, and distribution system, companies can develop optimal supply chains for every product or service they offer.

For example, Toyota was convinced that the market for the Prius, the hybrid car it launched in the United States in 2000, would be different from that of other models because it embodied new technologies and was in its infancy. The Japanese automobile maker had expertise in tracking U.S. trends and geographical preferences, but it felt that it would be difficult to predict consumer response to a hybrid car. Besides, the Prius might appeal to particular consumer segments, such as technophiles and conservationists, which Toyota didn't know much about. Convinced that the uncertainties were too great to allocate the Prius to dealers based on past trends, Toyota decided to keep inventory in central stockyards. Dealers took orders from consumers and communicated them via the Internet. Toyota shipped cars from stockyards, and dealers delivered them to buyers.

Although Toyota's transportation costs rose, it customized products to demand and managed inventory flawlessly. In 2002, for example, the number of Toyotas on the road in Northern California and the Southeast were 7% and 20%, respectively. However, Toyota sold 25% of its Prius output in Northern California and only 6% in the Southeast. Had Toyota not adapted its distribution system to the product, it would have faced stock outs in Northern California and been saddled with excess inventory in the Southeast, which may well have resulted in the product's failure.

Building an adaptable supply chain requires two key components: the ability to spot trends and the capability to change supply networks. To identify future patterns, it's necessary to follow some guidelines:

- Track economic changes, especially in developing countries, because as nations open up their economies to global competition, the costs, skills, and risks of global supply chain operations change. This liberalization results in the rise of specialized firms, and companies must periodically check to see if they can outsource more stages of operation. Before doing so, however, they must make sure that the infrastructure to link them with vendors and customers is in place. Global electronics vendors, such as Flextronics, Solectron, and Foxcom, have become adept at gathering data and adapting supply networks.

- Decipher the needs of your ultimate consumers—not just your immediate customers. Otherwise, you may fall victim to the "bullwhip effect," which amplifies and distorts demand fluctuations. For years, semiconductor manufacturers responded to customer forecasts and created gluts in markets. But when they started tracking demand for chip-based products, the manufacturers overcame the problem. For instance, in 2003, there were neither big inventory buildups nor shortages of semiconductors.

At the same time, companies must retain the option to alter supply chains. To do that, they must do two things:

- They must develop new suppliers that complement existing ones. When smart firms work in relatively unknown parts of the world, they use intermediaries like Li & Fung, the Hong Kong–based supply chain architects, to find reliable vendors.

- They must ensure that product design teams are aware of the supply chain implications of their designs. Designers must also be familiar with the three design-for-supply principles: commonality, which ensures that products share components; postponement, which delays the step at which products become different; and standardization, which ensures that components and processes for different products are the same. These principles allow firms to execute engineering changes whenever they adapt supply chains.

## Creating the Right Alignment

Great companies take care to align the interests of all the firms in their supply chain with their own. That's critical, because every firm—be it a supplier, an assembler, a distributor, or a retailer—tries to maximize only its own interests. (See "The Confinement of Nonalignment" at the end of this article.) If any company's interests differ from those of the other organizations in the supply chain, its actions will not maximize the chain's performance.

Misaligned interests can cause havoc even if supply chain partners are divisions of the same company, as HP discovered. In the late 1980s, HP's integrated circuit (IC) division tried to carry as little inventory as possible, partly because that was one of its key success factors. Those low inventory levels often resulted in long lead times in the supply of ICs to HP's ink-jet printer division. Since the division couldn't afford to keep customers waiting, it created a large inventory of printers to cope with the lead times in supplies. Both divisions were content, but from HP's viewpoint, it would have been far less expensive to have a greater inventory of lower-cost ICs and fewer stocks of expensive printers. That didn't happen, simply because HP's supply chain didn't align the interests of the divisions with those of the company.

Lack of alignment causes the failure of many supply chain practices. For example, several high-tech companies, including Flextronics, Solectron, Cisco, and 3Com, have set up supplier hubs close to their assembly plants. Vendors maintain just enough stock at the hubs to support manufacturers' needs, and they replenish the hubs without waiting for orders. Such vendor-managed inventory (VMI) systems allow suppliers to track the consumption of components, reduce transportation costs, and, since vendors can use the same hub to support several manufacturers, derive scale benefits. When VMI offers so many advantages, why hasn't it always reduced costs?

The problem starts with the fact that suppliers own components until they physically enter the manufacturers' assembly plants and therefore bear the costs of inventories for longer periods than they used to. Many suppliers are small and medium-sized companies that must borrow money to finance inventories at higher interest rates than large manufacturers pay. Thus, manufacturers have reduced costs by shifting the ownership of inventories to vendors, but supply chains bear higher costs because vendors' costs have risen. In fact, some VMI systems have generated friction because manufacturers have refused to share costs with vendors.

One way companies align their partners' interests with their own is by redefining the terms of their relationships so that firms share risks, costs, and rewards equitably. For instance, the world's largest printer, RR Donnelley (which prints HBR) recognized in the late 1990s that its supply chain performance relied heavily on paper-and-ink suppliers. If the quality and reliability of supplies improved, the company could reduce waste and make deliveries to customers on time. Like many other firms, RR Donnelley encouraged suppliers to come up with suggestions for improving processes and products. To align their interests with its own, however, the company also offered to split any resulting savings with suppliers. Not surprisingly, supplier-initiated improvements have helped enhance RR Donnelley's supply chain ever since.

Sometimes the process of alignment involves the use of intermediaries. In the case of VMI, for instance, some financial institutions now buy components from suppliers at hubs and sell them to manufacturers. Everyone benefits because the intermediaries' financing costs are lower than the vendors' costs. Although such an arrangement requires trust and commitment on the part of suppliers, financial intermediaries, and manufacturers, it is a powerful way to align the interests of companies in supply chains.

Automaker Saturn's service parts supply chain, one of the best in the industry, is a great example of incentive alignment that has led to outstanding results. Instead of causing heartburn, the system works well because Saturn aligned the interests of everyone in the chain—especially consumers.

Saturn has relieved car dealers of the burden of managing service parts inventories. The company uses a central system to make stocking and replenishment decisions for dealers, who have the right to accept, reject, or modify the company's suggestions. Saturn doesn't just monitor its performance in delivering service parts to dealers, even though that is the company's only responsibility. Instead, Saturn holds its managers and the dealers jointly accountable for the quality of service the vehicle owners experience. For example, the company tracks the off-the-shelf availability of parts at the dealers as the relevant metric. Saturn also measures its Service Parts Operation (SPO) division on the profits that dealers make from service parts as well as on the number of emergency orders that dealers place. That's because when a dealer doesn't have a part, Saturn transfers it from another dealer and bears the shipping costs. The SPO division can't overstock dealers because Saturn shares the costs of excess inventory with them. If no one buys a particular part from a dealer for nine months, Saturn will buy it back as obsolete inventory.

That kind of alignment produces two results. First, everyone in the chain has the same objective: to deliver the best service to consumers. While the off-the-shelf availability of service parts in the automobile industry ranges from 70% to 80%, service part availability at Saturn's dealers is 92.5%. After taking transfers from other retailers into account, the same-day availability of spare parts is actually 94%. Second, the right to decide about inventory replenishment rests with Saturn, which is in the best position to make those decisions. The company shares the risks of stock outs or overstocks with dealers, so it has an interest in making the best possible decisions. Fittingly, the inventory turnover (a measure of how efficient inventory management is, calculated by dividing the annual cost of inventory sold by the average inventory) of spare parts at Saturn's dealers is seven times a year while it is only between one and five times a year for other automobile companies' dealers.

Like Saturn, clever companies create alignment in supply chains in several ways. They start with the alignment of information, so that all the companies in a supply chain have equal access to forecasts, sales data, and plans. Next they align identities; in other words, the manufacturer must define the roles and responsibilities of each partner so that there is no scope for conflict. Then companies must align incentives, so that when companies try to maximize returns, they also maximize the supply chain's performance. To ensure that happens, companies must try to predict the possible behavior of supply chain partners in the light of their current incentives. Companies often perform such analyses to predict what competitors would do if they raised prices or entered a new segment; they need to do the same with their supply chain partners. Then they must redesign incentives so partners act in ways that are closer to what's best for the entire supply chain.

## Seven-Eleven Japan's Three Aces

Seven-Eleven Japan (SEJ) is an example of how a company that builds its supply chain on agility, adaptability, and alignment stays ahead of its rivals. The $21 billion convenience store chain has remarkably low stock out rates and in 2004 had an inventory turnover of 55. With gross profit margins of 30%, SEJ is also one of the most profitable retailers in the world. Just how has the 9,000-store retailer managed to sustain performance for more than a decade?

The company has designed its supply chain to respond to quick changes in demand—not to focus on fast or cheap deliveries. It has invested in real-time systems to detect changes in customer preference and tracks data on sales and consumers (gender and age) at every store. Well before the Internet era began, SEJ used satellite connections and ISDN lines to link all its stores with distribution centers, suppliers, and logistics providers. The data allow the supply chain to detect fluctuations in demand between stores, to alert suppliers to potential shifts in requirements, to help reallocate inventory among stores, and to ensure that the company restocks at the right time. SEJ schedules deliveries to each store within a ten-minute margin. If a truck is late by more than 30 minutes, the carrier has to pay a penalty equal to the gross margin of the products carried to the store. Employees reconfigure store shelves at least three times daily so that storefronts cater to different consumer segments and demands at different hours.

SEJ has adapted its supply chain to its strategy over time. Some years ago, the company decided to concentrate stores in key locations instead of building outlets all over the country. But doing so increased the possibility of traffic congestion every time the company replenished stores. The problem became more acute when SEJ decided to resupply stores three or more times a day. To minimize delays due to traffic snarls, the company adapted its distribution system. It asked its suppliers from the same region to consolidate shipments in a single truck instead of using several of them. That minimized the number of trucks going to its distribution centers, which is where SEJ cross-docks products for delivery to stores. The company has also expanded the kinds of vehicles it uses from trucks to motorcycles, boats, and even helicopters. The effectiveness of the company's logistics system is legendary. Less than six hours after the Kobe earthquake on January 17, 1995, when relief trucks were crawling at two miles per hour on the highways, SEJ used seven helicopters and 125 motorcycles to deliver 64,000 rice balls to the city.

Fundamental to the supply chain's operation is the close alignment between Seven-Eleven Japan's interests and those of its partners. The incentives and disincentives are clear: Make Seven-Eleven Japan successful, and share the rewards. Fail to deliver on time, and pay a penalty. That may seem harsh, but the company balances the equation by trusting its partners. For instance, when carriers deliver products to stores, no one verifies the truck's contents. That allows carriers to save time and money, since drivers don't have to wait after dropping off merchandise.

When Seven-Eleven Japan spots business opportunities, it works with suppliers to develop products and shares revenues with them. For instance, two years ago, SEJ created an e-commerce company, 7dream.com, with six partners. The new organization allows consumers to order products online or through kiosks at SEJ stores and pick up the merchandise at any Seven-Eleven. The partners benefit from SEJ's logistics network, which delivers products to stores efficiently, as well as from the convenient location of stores. By encouraging partners to set up multimedia kiosks to produce games, tickets, or CDs in its shops, Seven-Eleven Japan has become a manufacturing outlet for partners. The company could not have aligned the interests of its partners more closely with those of its own.

WHEN I DESCRIBE THE triple-A supply chain to companies, most of them immediately assume it will require more technology and investment. Nothing could be further from the truth. Most firms already have the infrastructure in place to create triple-A supply chains. What they need is a fresh attitude and a new culture to get their supply chains to deliver triple-A performance. Companies must give up the efficiency mind-set, which is counterproductive; be prepared to keep changing networks; and, instead of looking out for their interests alone, take responsibility for the entire chain. This can be challenging for companies because there are no technologies that can do those things; only managers can make them happen.

---

## Building the Triple-A Supply Chain

### Agility

*Objectives:*

RESPOND TO SHORT-TERM CHANGES in demand or supply quickly; handle external disruptions smoothly.

### *Methods:*

- Promote flow of information with suppliers and customers.
- Develop collaborative relationships with suppliers.
- Design for postponement.

- Build inventory buffers by maintaining a stockpile of inexpensive but key components.
- Have a dependable logistics system or partner.
- Draw up contingency plans and develop crisis management teams.

### Adaptability

#### Objectives:

ADJUST SUPPLY CHAIN'S DESIGN TO meet structural shifts in markets; modify supply network to strategies, products, and technologies.

#### Methods:

- Monitor economies all over the world to spot new supply bases and markets.
- Use intermediaries to develop fresh suppliers and logistics infrastructure.
- Evaluate needs of ultimate consumers—not just immediate customers.
- Create flexible product designs.
- Determine where companies' products stand in terms of technology cycles and product life cycles.

### Alignment

#### Objective:

CREATE INCENTIVES for better performance.

#### Methods:

- Exchange information and knowledge freely with vendors and customers.
- Lay down roles, tasks, and responsibilities clearly for suppliers and customers.

- Equitably share risks, costs, and gains of improvement initiatives.

---

## The Importance of Being Agile

MOST COMPANIES OVERLOOK the idea that supply chains should be agile. That's understandable; adaptability and alignment are more novel concepts than agility is. However, even if your supply chain is both adaptable and aligned, it's dangerous to disregard agility.

In 1995, Hewlett-Packard teamed up with Canon to design and launch ink-jet printers. At the outset, the American company aligned its interests with those of its Japanese partner. While HP took on the responsibility of producing printed circuit boards (or "formaters"), Canon agreed to manufacture engines for the LaserJet series. That was an equitable division of responsibilities, and the two R&D teams learned to work together closely. After launching the LaserJet, HP and Canon quickly adapted the supply network to the product's markets. HP used its manufacturing facilities in Idaho and Italy to support the LaserJet, and Canon used plants in West Virginia and Tokyo.

But HP and Canon failed to anticipate one problem. To keep costs down, Canon agreed to alter the number of engines it produced, but only if HP communicated changes well in advance—say, six or more months before printers entered the market. However, HP could estimate demand accurately only three or fewer months before printers hit the market. At that stage, Canon could modify its manufacturing schedule by just a few percentage points. As a result, the supply chain couldn't cope with sudden fluctuations in demand. So when there was an unexpected drop in demand for the LaserJet III toward the end of its life cycle, HP was stuck with a huge and expensive surplus of printer engines: the infamous Laser-Jet mountain. Having an adaptable and aligned supply chain didn't help HP overcome its lack of agility.

## Adaptation of the Fittest

MANY EXECUTIVES ASK ME, with a twinkle in their eye, if companies must really keep adapting supply chains. Companies may find it tough to accept the idea that they have to keep changing, but they really have no choice.

Just ask Lucent. In the mid-1990s, when the American telecommunications giant realized that it could make inroads in Asia only if had local manufacturing facilities, it overhauled its supply chain. Lucent set up plants in Taiwan and China, which allowed the company to customize switches as inexpensively and quickly as rivals Siemens and Alcatel could. To align the interests of parent and subsidiaries, Lucent executives stopped charging the Asian ventures inflated prices for modules that the company shipped from the United States. By the late 1990s, Lucent had recaptured market share in China, Taiwan, India, and Indonesia.

Unhappily, the story doesn't end there, because Lucent stopped adapting its supply chain. The company didn't realize that many medium-sized manufacturers had developed the technology and expertise to produce components and subassemblies for digital switches and that because of economies of scale, they could do so at a fraction of the integrated manufacturers' costs. Realizing where the future lay, competitors aggressively outsourced the manufacture of switching systems. Because of the resulting cost savings, they were able to quote lower prices than Lucent. Meanwhile, Lucent was reluctant to outsource its manufacturing because it had invested in its own factories. Ultimately, however, Lucent had no option but to shut down its Taiwan factory in 2002 and create an outsourced supply chain. The company's adaptation came too late for Lucent to regain control of the global market, even though the supply chain was agile and aligned.

---

## The Confinement of Nonalignment

IT'S NOT EASY FOR EXECUTIVES TO accept that different firms in the same supply chain can have different interests, or that interest nonalignment can lead to inventory problems as dire as those that may arise through a lack of agility or a lack of adaptability. But the story of Cisco's supply chain clinches the argument.

All through the 1990s, everyone regarded Cisco's supply chain as almost infallible. The company was among the first to make use of the Internet to communicate with suppliers and customers, automate work flows among trading partners, and use solutions such as remote product testing, which allowed suppliers to deliver quality results with a minimum of manual input. Cisco outsourced the manufacturing of most of its networking products and worked closely with contract manufacturers to select the right locations to support its needs. If ever there were a supply chain that was agile and adaptable, Cisco's was it.

Why then did Cisco have to write off $2.25 billion of inventory in 2001? There were several factors at play, but the main culprit was the misalignment of Cisco's interests with those of its contract manufacturers. The contractors accumulated a large amount of inventory for months without factoring in the demand for Cisco's products. Even when the growth of the U.S. economy slowed down, the contractors continued to produce and store inventory at the same pace. Finally, Cisco found it couldn't use most of the inventory of raw materials because demand had fallen sharply. The company had to sell the raw materials off as scrap.

**Originally published in October 2004**
**Reprint R0410F**

# Decoding the DNA of the Toyota Production System

STEVEN J. SPEAR AND H. KENT BOWEN

## Executive Summary

THE TOYOTA PRODUCTION SYSTEM is a paradox. On the one hand, every activity, connection, and production flow in a Toyota factory is rigidly scripted. Yet at the same time, Toyota's operations are enormously flexible and responsive to customer demand. How can that be?

After an extensive four-year study of the system in more than 40 plants, the authors came to understand that at Toyota it's the very rigidity of the operations that makes the flexibility possible. That's because the company's operations can be seen as a continuous series of controlled experiments. Whenever Toyota defines a specification, it is establishing a hypothesis that is then tested through action. This approach—the scientific method—is not imposed on workers, it's ingrained in them. And it stimulates them to engage in the kind of

117

experimentation that is widely recognized as the corner-stone of a learning organization.

The Toyota Production System grew out of the work-ings of the company over 50 years, and it has never actually been written down. Making the implicit explicit, the authors lay out four principles that show how Toyota sets up all its operations as experiments and teaches the scientific method to its workers. The first rule governs the way workers do their work. The second, the way they interact with one another. The third governs how produc-tion lines are constructed. And the last, how people learn to improve. Every activity, connection, and production path designed according to these rules must have built-in tests that signal problems immediately. And it is the con-tinual response to those problems that makes this seem-ingly rigid system so flexible and adaptive to changing circumstances.

---

THE TOYOTA PRODUCTION SYSTEM has long been hailed as the source of Toyota's outstanding performance as a manufacturer. The system's distinctive practices—its kanban cards and quality circles, for instance—have been widely introduced elsewhere. Indeed, following their own internal efforts to benchmark the world's best manufac-turing companies, GM, Ford, and Chrysler have indepen-dently created major initiatives to develop Toyota-like production systems. Companies that have tried to adopt the system can be found in fields as diverse as aerospace, consumer products, metals processing, and industrial products.

What's curious is that few manufacturers have man-aged to imitate Toyota successfully—even though the

company has been extraordinarily open about its practices. Hundreds of thousands of executives from thousands of businesses have toured Toyota's plants in Japan
and the United States. Frustrated by their inability to
replicate Toyota's performance, many visitors assume
that the secret of Toyota's success must lie in its cultural
roots. But that's just not the case. Other Japanese companies, such as Nissan and Honda, have fallen short of Toyota's standards, and Toyota has successfully introduced
its production system all around the world, including in
North America, where the company is this year building
over a million cars, minivans, and light trucks.

So why has it been so difficult to decode the Toyota
Production System? The answer, we believe, is that
observers confuse the tools and practices they see on
their plant visits with the system itself. That makes it
impossible for them to resolve an apparent paradox of
the system—namely, that activities, connections, and
production flows in a Toyota factory are rigidly scripted,
yet at the same time Toyota's operations are enormously
flexible and adaptable. Activities and processes are constantly being challenged and pushed to a higher level of
performance, enabling the company to continually innovate and improve.

To understand Toyota's success, you have to unravel
the paradox—you have to see that the rigid specification
is the very thing that makes the flexibility and creativity
possible. That's what we came to realize after an extensive, four-year study of the Toyota Production System in
which we examined the inner workings of more than
40 plants in the United States, Europe, and Japan, some
operating according to the system, some not. We studied
both process and discrete manufacturers whose products
ranged from prefabricated housing, auto parts and final

auto assembly, cell phones, and computer printers to injection-molded plastics and aluminum extrusions. We studied not only routine production work but also service functions like equipment maintenance, workers' training and supervision, logistics and materials handling, and process design and redesign.

We found that, for outsiders, the key is to understand that the Toyota Production System creates a community of scientists. Whenever Toyota defines a specification, it is establishing sets of hypotheses that can then be tested. In other words, it is following the scientific method. To make any changes, Toyota uses a rigorous problem-solving process that requires a detailed assessment of the current state of affairs and a plan for improvement that is, in effect, an experimental test of the proposed changes. With anything less than such scientific rigor, change at Toyota would amount to little more than random trial and error—a blindfolded walk through life.

The fact that the scientific method is so ingrained at Toyota explains why the high degree of specification and structure at the company does not promote the command and control environment one might expect. Indeed, in watching people doing their jobs and in helping to design production processes, we learned that the system actually stimulates workers and managers to engage in the kind of experimentation that is widely recognized as the cornerstone of a learning organization. That is what distinguishes Toyota from all the other companies we studied.

The Toyota Production System and the scientific method that underpins it were not imposed on Toyota— they were not even chosen consciously. The system grew naturally out of the workings of the company over five mon sense of what the ideal production system would be, and that shared vision motivates them to make improvements beyond what would be necessary merely to meet the current needs of their customers. This notion of the ideal is very pervasive, and we believe it is essential to understanding the Toyota Production System.

When they speak of the ideal, workers at Toyota do not mean something philosophically abstract. They have a concrete definition in mind, one that is remarkably consistent throughout the company. Very specifically, for Toyota's workers, the output of an ideal person, group of people, or machine:

- is defect free (that it, it has the features and performance the customer expects);

- can be delivered one request at a time (a batch size of one);

- can be supplied on demand in the version requested;

- can be delivered immediately;

- can be produced without wasting any materials, labor, energy, or other resources (such as costs associated with inventory); and

- can be produced in a work environment that is safe physically, emotionally, and professionally for every employee.

We consistently found people at plants that used the Toyota Production System making changes that pushed operations toward this ideal. At one company that produced electromechanical products, for example, we found that workers had come up with a number of ingenious error-detecting gauges that generated a simple, unambiguous yes-or-no signal to indicate whether their decades. As a result, it has never been written down, and Toyota's workers often are not able to articulate it. That's why it's so hard for outsiders to grasp. In this article, we attempt to lay out how Toyota's system works. We try to make explicit what is implicit. We describe four principles—three rules of design, which show how Toyota sets up all its operations as experiments, and one rule of improvement, which describes how Toyota teaches the scientific method to workers at every level of the organization. It is these rules—and not the specific practices and tools that people observe during their plant visits—that in our opinion form the essence of Toyota's system. That is why we think of the rules as the DNA of the Toyota Production System. Let's take a closer look at those rules (for a summary, see "The Four Rules" at the end of this article and the exhibit "The Experiments of the Toyota Production System").

## Rule 1: How People Work

Toyota's managers recognize that the devil is in the details; that's why they ensure that all work is highly specified as to content, sequence, timing, and outcome. When a car's seat is installed, for instance, the bolts are always tightened in the same order, the time it takes to turn each bolt is specified, and so is the torque to which the bolt should be tightened. Such exactness is applied not only to the repetitive motions of production workers but also to the activities of all people regardless of their functional specialty or hierarchical role. The requirement that every activity be specified is the first unstated rule of the system. Put this baldly, the rule seems simple, something you'd expect everyone to understand and be

# The Experiments of the Toyota Production System

*When organizations are managed according to the four rules, individuals are repeatedly conducting experiments, testing in operation the hypotheses built into the designs of individual work activities, customer-supplier connections, pathways, and improvement efforts. The hypotheses, the way they are tested, and the response if they are refuted are summarized below.*

| Rule | Hypotheses | Signs of a problem | Responses |
|------|-----------|-------------------|-----------|
| 1 | The person or machine can do the activity as specified. | The activity is not done as specified. | Determine the true skill level of the person or the true capability of the machine and train or modify as appropriate. |
| | If the activity is done as specified, the good or service will be defect free. | The outcome is defective. | Modify the design activity. |
| 2 | Customers' requests will be for goods and services in a specific mix and volume. | Responses don't keep pace with requests. | Determine the true mix and volume of demand and the true capability of the supplier; retrain, modify activities, or reassign customer-supplier pairs as appropriate. |
| | The supplier can respond to customers' requests. | The supplier is idle, waiting for requests. | |

| 3 | Every supplier that is connected to the flow path is required. | A person or machine is not actually needed. | Determine why the supplier was unnecessary, and redesign the flow path. |
| | Any supplier not connected to the flow path is not needed. | A nonspecified supplier provides an intermediate good or service. | Learn why the nonspecified supplier was actually required, and redesign the flow path. |
| 4 | A specific change in an activity, connection, or flow path will improve cost, quality, lead time, batch size, or safety by a specific amount. | The actual result is different from the expected result. | Learn how the activity was actually performed or the connection or flow path was actually operated. Determine the true effects of the change. Redesign the change. |

able to follow easily. But in reality, most managers outside Toyota and its partners don't take this approach
to work design and execution—even when they think
they do.

Let's look at how operators at a typical U.S. auto plant
install the front passenger seat into a car. They are supposed to take four bolts from a cardboard box, carry
them and a torque wrench to the car, tighten the four
bolts, and enter a code into a computer to indicate that
the work has been done without problems. Then they
wait for the next car to arrive. New operators are usually
trained by experienced workers, who teach by demon-
strating what to do. A seasoned colleague might be available to help a new operator with any difficulties, such as
failing to tighten a bolt enough or forgetting to enter the
computer code.

This sounds straightforward, so what's wrong with it?
The problem is that those specifications actually allow—
and even assume—considerable variation in the way
employees do their work. Without anyone realizing it,
there is plenty of scope for a new operator to put the
seat into the vehicle differently than an experienced
employee would. Some operators might put the front
bolts in after the rear bolts; some might do it the other
way around. Some operators might put each bolt in and
then tighten them all; others might tighten as they go
along. All this variation translates into poorer quality,
lower productivity, and higher costs. More important, it
hinders learning and improvement in the organization
because the variations hide the link between how the
work is done and the results.

At Toyota's plants, because operators (new and old,
junior and supervisory) follow a well-defined sequence of
steps for a particular job, it is instantly clear when they
deviate from the specifications. Consider how workers at

Toyota's Georgetown, Kentucky, plant install the right-front seat into a Camry. The work is designed as a sequence of seven tasks, all of which are expected to be completed in 55 seconds as the car moves at a fixed speed through a worker's zone. If the production worker finds himself doing task 6 (installing the rear seat-bolts) before task 4 (installing the front seat-bolts), then the job is actually being done differently than it was designed to be done, indicating that something must be wrong. Similarly, if after 40 seconds the worker is still on task 4, which should have been completed after 31 seconds, then something, too, is amiss. To make problem detection even simpler, the length of the floor for each work area is marked in tenths. So if the worker is passing the sixth of the ten floor marks (that is, if he is 33 seconds into the cycle) and is still on task 4, then he and his team leader know that he has fallen behind. Since the deviation is immediately apparent, worker and supervisor can move to correct the problem right away and then determine how to change the specifications or retrain the worker to prevent a recurrence. (See "How Toyota's Workers Learn the Rules" at the end of this article for a short description of the process by which workers learn how to design work in this way.)

Even complex and infrequent activities, such as training an inexperienced workforce at a new plant, launching a new model, changing over a production line, or shifting equipment from one part of a plant to another, are designed according to this rule. At one of Toyota's suppliers in Japan, for example, equipment from one area of the plant was moved to create a new production line in response to changes in demand for certain products. Moving the machinery was broken into 14 separate activities. Each activity was then further subdivided and designed as a series of tasks. A specific person was assigned to do each task in a specified sequence. As each of the machines was moved, the way the tasks were actually done was compared with what was expected according to the original design, and discrepancies were immediately signaled.

In calling for people to do their work as a highly specified sequence of steps, rule 1 forces them to test hypotheses through action. Performing the activity tests the two hypotheses implicit in its design: first, that the person doing the activity is capable of performing it correctly and, second, that performing the activity actually creates the expected outcome. Remember the seat installer? If he can't insert the seat in the specified way within the specified amount of time, then he is clearly refuting at least one of these two hypotheses, thereby indicating that the activity needs to be redesigned or the worker needs to be trained.

## Rule 2: How People Connect

Where the first rule explains how people perform their individual work activities, the second rule explains how they connect with one another. We express this rule as follows: every connection must be standardized and direct, unambiguously specifying the people involved, the form and quantity of the goods and services to be provided, the way requests are made by each customer, and the expected time in which the requests will be met. The rule creates a supplier-customer relationship between each person and the individual who is responsible for providing that person with each specific good or service. As a result, there are no gray zones in deciding who provides what to whom and when. When a worker makes a request for parts, there is no confusion about the supplier, the number of units required, or the timing of the delivery. Similarly, when a person needs assistance, there is no confusion over who will provide it, how the help will be triggered, and what services will be delivered.

The real question that concerns us here is whether people interact differently at Toyota than they do at other companies. Let's return to our seat installer. When he needs a new container of plastic bolt covers, he gives a request to a materials handler, who is the designated bolt-cover supplier. Commonly, such a request is made with a kanban, a laminated card that specifies the part's identification number, the quantity of parts in the container, and the locations of the part supplier and of the worker (the customer) who will install it. At Toyota, kanban cards and other devices like *andon* cords set up direct links between the suppliers and the customers. The connections are as smooth as the passing of the baton in the best Olympic relay teams because they are just as carefully thought out and executed. For example, the number of parts in a container and the number of containers in circulation for any given part are determined by the physical realities of the production system—the distances, the changeover times, and so on. Likewise, the number of workers per team is determined by the types of problems expected to occur, the level of assistance the team members need, and the skills and capabilities of the team's leader.

Other companies devote substantial resources to coordinating people, but their connections generally aren't so direct and unambiguous. In most plants, requests for materials or assistance often take a convoluted route from the line worker to the supplier via an intermediary. Any supervisor can answer any call for help because a specific person has not been assigned.

The disadvantage of that approach, as Toyota recognizes, is that when something is everyone's problem it becomes no one's problem.

The requirement that people respond to supply requests within a specific time frame further reduces the possibility of variance. That is especially true in service requests. A worker encountering a problem is expected to ask for assistance at once. The designated assistant is then expected to respond immediately and resolve the problem within the worker's cycle time. If the worker is installing a front seat every 55 seconds, say, then a request for help must be answered and dealt with in less than the 55 seconds. If the problem cannot be resolved in less than 55 seconds, that failure immediately challenges the hypotheses in this customer-supplier connection for assistance. Perhaps the request signal is ambiguous. Perhaps the designated assistant has too many other requests for help and is busy or is not a capable problem solver. Constantly testing the hypotheses in this way keeps the system flexible, making it possible to adjust the system continually and constructively.

The striking thing about the requirement to ask for help at once is that it is often counterintuitive to managers who are accustomed to encouraging workers to try to resolve problems on their own before calling for help. But then problems remain hidden and are neither shared nor resolved company-wide. The situation is made worse if workers begin to solve problems themselves and then arbitrarily decide when the problem is big enough to warrant a call for help. Problems mount up and only get solved much later, by which time valuable information about the real causes of the problem may have been lost.

# Rule 3: How the Production Line Is Constructed

All production lines at Toyota have to be set up so that every product and service flows along a simple, specified path. That path should not change unless the production line is expressly redesigned. In principle, then, there are no forks or loops to convolute the flow in any of Toyota's supply chains. That's the third rule.

To get a concrete idea of what that means, let's return to our seat installer. If he needs more plastic bolt covers, he orders them from the specific material handler responsible for providing him with bolt covers. That designated supplier makes requests to his own designated supplier at the off-line store in the factory who, in turn, makes requests directly to his designated supplier at the bolt cover factory's shipping dock. In this way, the production line links each person who contributes to the production and delivery of the product, from the Toyota factory, through the molding company, to even the plastic pellet manufacturer.

The point is that when production lines are designed in accordance with rule 3, goods and services do not flow to the next available person or machine but to a *specific* person or machine. If for some reason that person or machine is not available, Toyota will see it as a problem that might require the line to be redesigned.

The stipulation that every product follow a simple, prespecified path doesn't mean that each path is dedicated to only one particular product, however. Quite the contrary: each production line at a Toyota plant typically accommodates many more types of products than its counterparts do at other companies.

The third rule doesn't apply only to products—it applies to services, like help requests, as well. If our seat installer, for example, needs help, that too comes from a single, specified supplier. And if that supplier can't provide the necessary assistance, she, in turn, has a designated helper. In some of Toyota's plants, this pathway for assistance is three, four, or five links long, connecting the shop floor worker to the plant manager.

The third rule runs contrary to conventional wisdom about production lines and pooling resources—even contrary to how most people think the Toyota Production System works. According to received wisdom, as a product or service is passed down the line, it should go to the next machine or person available to process it further. Similarly, most people assume that help should come from the first available person rather than from a specific person. At one auto parts supplier we studied, for example, most of the parts could be stamped on more than one press machine and welded at more than one welding station. Before the company adopted the Toyota system, its practice was to pass each part on to the first available press machine and to the first available welder. When the plant switched over, under Toyota's guidance, each type of part followed only one production path through the plant.

By requiring that every pathway be specified, the rule ensures that an experiment will occur each time the path is used. Here the hypotheses embedded in a pathway designed according to rule 3 are that every supplier connected to the pathway is necessary, and any supplier not connected is not necessary. If workers at the auto parts supplier found themselves wanting to divert production to another machine or welding station, or if they began turning for help to someone other than their designated helpers, they'd conclude that their actual demand or capacity didn't match their expectations. And there would also be no ambiguity about which press or welder was involved. Again, the workers would revisit the design of their production line. Thus rule 3, like rules 1 and 2, enables Toyota to conduct experiments and remain flexible and responsive.

## Rule 4: How to Improve

Identifying problems is just the first step. For people to consistently make effective changes, they must know how to change and who is responsible for making the changes. Toyota explicitly teaches people how to improve, not expecting them to learn strictly from personal experience. That's where the rule for improvement comes in. Specifically, rule 4 stipulates that any improvement to production activities, to connections between workers or machines, or to pathways must be made in accordance with the scientific method, under the guidance of a teacher, and at the lowest possible organizational level. Let's look first at how Toyota's people learn the scientific method.

### HOW PEOPLE LEARN TO IMPROVE

In 1986, Aisin Seiki, a Toyota Group company that made complex products such as power trains for the auto industry, created a line to manufacture mattresses to absorb excess capacity in one of its plants. Since 1986, its range has grown from 200 to 850 types of mattresses, its volume has grown from 160 mattresses per day to 550, and its productivity has doubled. Here's an example of how they did it.

On one of our visits to this plant, we studied a team of mattress assembly workers who were being taught to improve their problem-solving skills by redesigning their own work. Initially, the workers had been responsible for doing only their own standardized work; they had not been responsible for solving problems. Then the workers were assigned a leader who trained them to frame problems better and to formulate and test hypotheses—in other words, he taught them how to use the scientific method to design their team's work in accordance with the first three rules. The results were impressive. One of the team's accomplishments, for instance, was to redesign the way edging tape was attached to the mattresses, thereby reducing the defect rate by 90%. (See the exhibit "On-Demand Production at the Aisin Mattress Factory.")

To make changes, people are expected to present the explicit logic of the hypotheses. Let's look at what that can involve. Hajime Ohba, general manager of the Toyota Supplier Support Center, was visiting a factory in which one of TSSC's consultants was leading a training and improvement activity (for a description of the role of the Toyota Production System promotion centers, see "Toyota's Commitment to Learning" at the end of this article). The consultant was helping factory employees and their supervisor reduce the manufacturing lead time of a particular line, and Ohba was there to evaluate the group's progress.

Group members began their presentation by describing the steps by which their product was created—delineating all the problems they identified when they had first studied the process for changing over a machine from making one part to making another, and explaining the specific changes they had made in response to each of those problems. They concluded by saying, "When we started, the changeover required 15 minutes. We were hoping to reduce that by two-thirds—to achieve a five-minute changeover—so that we could reduce batch sizes by two-thirds. Because of the modifications we made, we achieved a changeover time of seven and a half minutes—a reduction of one-half."

After their presentation, Ohba asked why the group members had not achieved the five-minute goal they had originally established. They were a bit taken aback. After all, they had reduced the changeover time by 50%, yet Ohba's question suggested he had seen opportunities for even greater improvement that they had missed. They offered explanations having to do with machine

---

### On-Demand Production at the Aisin Mattress Factory

*Aisin Seiki produces 850 varieties of mattresses, distinguished by size, firmness, covering fabric, quilting pattern, and edge trim. Customers can order any one of these in a retail store and have it delivered to their homes in three days, yet Aisin maintains an inventory at the plant equal to just 1.5 days of demand. To be able to do so, Aisin has made thousands of changes in individual work activities, in the connections linking customers and suppliers of intermediate goods and services, and to the overall production lines. This table captures how dramatic the results of those changes have been.*

|                                   | 1986 | 1988 | 1992 | 1996 | 1997 |
|-----------------------------------|------|------|------|------|------|
| Styles                            | 200  | 325  | 670  | 750  | 850  |
| Units per day                     | 160  | 230  | 360  | 530  | 550  |
| Units per person                  | 8    | 11   | 13   | 20   | 26   |
| Productivity index                | 100  | 138  | 175  | 197  | 208  |
| Finished-goods inventory (days)   | 30   | 2.5  | 1.8  | 1.5  | 1.5  |
| Number of assembly lines          | 2    | 2    | 3    | 3    | 2    |

complexity, technical difficulty, and equipment upgrade costs. Ohba responded to these replies with yet more questions, each one meant to push the consultant and the factory people to articulate and challenge their most basic assumptions about what could and could not be changed—assumptions that both guided and constrained the way they had solved their problems. Were they sure four bolts were necessary? Might the changeover be accomplished with two? Were they certain that all the steps they included in the changeover were needed? Might some be combined or eliminated? In asking why they had not achieved the five-minute goal, Ohba was not suggesting that the team had failed. Rather, he was trying to get them to realize that they had not fully explored all their improvement opportunities because they had not questioned their assumptions deeply enough.

There was a second reason for Ohba's persistence. He was trying to show the group members that their improvement activity had not been carried out as a bona fide experiment. They had established a goal of five minutes based on the premise that faster changeovers and smaller batches are better than slower changeovers and larger batches. But here they were confusing goals with predictions based on hypotheses. The goal was not a prediction of what they believed they would achieve through the specific improvement steps they planned to take. As a result, they had not designed the improvement effort as an experiment with an explicit, clearly articulated, verifiable hypothesis of the form, "If we make the following specific changes, we expect to achieve this specific outcome." Although they had reduced the changeover time considerably, they had not tested the hypotheses implicit in their effort. For Ohba, it was critical that the workers and their supervisor realize that how they made changes was as important as what changes they made.

## WHO DOES THE IMPROVEMENT

Frontline workers make the improvements to their own jobs, and their supervisors provide direction and assistance as teachers. If something is wrong with the way a worker connects with a particular supplier within the immediate assembly area, the two of them make improvements, with the assistance of their common supervisor. The Aisin team we described earlier, for example, consisted of the assembly line workers and the supervisor, who was also their instructor. When changes are made on a larger scale, Toyota ensures that improvement teams are created consisting of the people who are directly affected and the person responsible for supervising the pathways involved.

Thus the process remains the same even at the highest levels. At Aisin's mattress factory, we found that the plant manager took responsibility for leading the change from three production lines back to two (the number had risen to three to cope with an increase in product types). He was involved not just because it was a big change but also because he had operational responsibility for overseeing the way work flowed from the feeder lines to the final assembly lines. In this way, Toyota ensures that problem solving and learning take place at all levels of the company. Of course, as we have already seen, Toyota will bring in external experts as necessary to ensure the quality of the learning process.

In the long term, the organizational structures of companies that follow the Toyota Production System will shift to adapt to the nature and frequency of the problems they encounter. Since the organizational changes are usually being made at a very low level, however, they can be hard for outsiders to detect. That's because it is the nature of the problems that determines who should solve them and how the organization is designed. One consequence is that different organizational structures coexist quite happily even in the same plant.

Consider Toyota's engine-machining plant in Kamigo, Japan. The plant has two machine divisions, each of which has three independent production shops. When we visited in summer 1998, the production people in the first machine division answered to shop heads, and the process engineers answered directly to the head of the division. However, in the second machine division, the engineers were distributed among the three shops and, like the production workers, answered to the various shop heads. Neither organizational structure is inherently superior. Rather, the people we interviewed explained, problems in the first division happened to create a situation that required the engineers to learn from one another and to pool engineering resources. By contrast, the problems that arose in the second division required the production and engineering people to cooperate at the level of the individual shops. Thus the organizational differences reflect the fact that the two divisions encountered different problems.

## Toyota's Notion of the Ideal

By inculcating the scientific method at all levels of the workforce, Toyota ensures that people will clearly state the expectations they will be testing when they implement the changes they have planned. But beyond this, we found that people in companies following the Toyota Production System share a common goal. They have a com-

output was free of defects—as specified in the ideal. At yet another plant, which manufactures injection-molded parts, we found that workers had reduced the time it took to change a large molding die from an already speedy five minutes to three minutes. This allowed the company to reduce the batch sizes of each part it produced by 40%, bringing it closer to the ideal batch size of one. As Toyota moves toward the ideal, it may temporarily hold one of its dimensions to be more important than another. Sometimes this can result in practices that go against the popular view of Toyota's operations. We have seen cases where Toyota keeps higher levels of inventory or produces in batch sizes larger than observers generally expect of a just-in-time operation, as we describe in "Countermeasures in the Toyota Production System" at the end of this article.

Toyota's ideal state shares many features of the popular notion of mass customization—the ability to create virtually infinite variations of a product as efficiently as possible and at the lowest possible cost. In the final analysis, Toyota's ideal plant would indeed be one where a Toyota customer could drive up to a shipping dock, ask for a customized product or service, and get it at once at the lowest possible price and with no defects. To the extent that a Toyota plant—or a Toyota worker's activity—falls short of this ideal, that shortcoming is a source of creative tension for further improvement efforts.

## The Organizational Impact of the Rules

If the rules make companies using the Toyota Production System a community of scientists performing continual experiments, then why aren't these organizations in a state of chaos? Why can one person make a change without adversely affecting the work of other people on the production line? How can Toyota constantly introduce changes to its operations while keeping them running at full tilt? In other words, how does Toyota improve and remain stable at the same time?

Once again, the answer is in the rules. By making people capable of and responsible for doing and improving their own work, by standardizing connections between individual customers and suppliers, and by pushing the resolution of connection and flow problems to the lowest possible level, the rules create an organization with a nested modular structure, rather like traditional Russian dolls that come one inside the other. The great benefit of nested, modular organizations is that people can implement design changes in one part without unduly affecting other parts. That's why managers at Toyota can delegate so much responsibility without creating chaos. Other companies that follow the rules will also find it possible to change without experiencing undue disruption.

Of course, the structures of other companies have features in common with those that follow the Toyota Production System, but in our research we found no company that had them all that did not follow the system. It may turn out in the end that you can build the structure only by investing the time Toyota has. But we believe that if a company dedicates itself to mastering the rules, it has a better chance of replicating Toyota's DNA—and with that, its performance.

## The Four Rules

THE TACIT KNOWLEDGE THAT underlies the Toyota Production System can be captured in four basic rules. These rules guide the design, operation, and improvement of every activity, connection, and pathway for every product and service. The rules are as follows:

**Rule 1:**   All work shall be highly specified as to content, sequence, timing, and outcome.

**Rule 2:**   Every customer-supplier connection must be direct, and there must be an unambiguous yes-or-no way to send requests and receive responses.

**Rule 3:**   The pathway for every product and service must be simple and direct.

**Rule 4:**   Any improvement must be made in accordance with the scientific method, under the guidance of a teacher, at the lowest possible level in the organization.

All the rules require that activities, connections, and flow paths have built-in tests to signal problems automatically. It is the continual response to problems that makes this seemingly rigid system so flexible and adaptable to changing circumstances.

## How Toyota's Workers Learn the Rules

IF THE RULES OF THE Toyota Production System aren't explicit, how are they transmitted? Toyota's managers don't tell workers and supervisors specifically how to do their work. Rather, they use a teaching and learning approach that allows their workers to discover the rules as a consequence of solving problems. For example, the supervisor teaching a person the principles of the first rule will come to the work site and, while the person is doing his or her job, ask a series of questions:

- How do you do this work?
- How do you know you are doing this work correctly?
- How do you know that the outcome is free of defects?
- What do you do if you have a problem?

This continuing process gives the person increasingly deeper insights into his or her own specific work. From many experiences of this sort, the person gradually learns to generalize how to design all activities according to the principles embodied in rule 1.

All the rules are taught in a similar Socratic fashion of iterative questioning and problem solving. Although this method is particularly effective for teaching, it leads to knowledge that is implicit. Consequently, the Toyota Production System has so far been transferred successfully only when managers have been able and willing to engage in a similar process of questioning to facilitate learning by doing.

## Toyota's Commitment to Learning

ALL THE ORGANIZATIONS WE STUDIED that are managed according to the Toyota Production System share an overarching belief that people are the most significant corporate asset and that investments in their knowledge and skills are necessary to build competitiveness. That's why at these organizations all managers are expected to be able to do the jobs of everyone they supervise and also to teach their workers how to solve problems according to the scientific method. The leadership model applies as much to the first-level "team leader" supervisors as it does to those at the top of the organization. In that way, everybody at Toyota shares in the development of human resources. In effect, there is a cascading pathway for teaching, which starts with the plant manager, that delivers training to each employee.

To reinforce the learning and improvement process, each plant and major business unit in the Toyota Group employs a number of Toyota Production System consultants whose primary responsibility is to help senior managers move their organizations toward the ideal. These "learner-leader-teachers" do so by identifying ever more subtle and difficult problems and by teaching people how to solve problems scientifically.

Many of these individuals have received intensive training at Toyota's Operations Management Consulting Division. OMCD was established in Japan as an outgrowth of efforts by Taiichi Ohno—one of the original architects of the Toyota Production System—to develop and diffuse the system throughout Toyota and its suppliers. Many of Toyota's top officers—including Toyota Motor's new president, Fujio Cho—have honed their skills within OMCD. During their OMCD tenure, which can extend for a period of years, Toyota's employees are relieved of all line responsibilities and instead are charged with leading improvement and training activities in the plants of Toyota and its suppliers. By supporting all of Toyota's plant and logistical operations in this way, OMCD serves as a training center, building its consultants' expertise by giving them opportunities to solve many difficult problems and teach others to do the same.

In 1992, Toyota founded the Toyota Supplier Support Center (TSSC) in the United States to provide North American companies with training in the Toyota Production System. Modeled on OMCD, TSSC has given workshops to more than 140 companies and direct assistance to 80. Although most of these companies are auto suppliers, few are exclusively Toyota suppliers; participants come from other industries and from universities, government organizations, and industry associations. Indeed, much of the research for this paper was derived from the experience of one of the authors, who was a member of a TSSC team for five months, promoting the Toyota Production System at a plant that supplies Toyota and two other auto assembly plants.

## Countermeasures in the Toyota Production System

TOYOTA DOES NOT CONSIDER any of the tools or practices—such as kanbans or *andon* cords, which so many outsiders have observed and copied—as fundamental to the Toyota Production System. Toyota uses them merely as temporary responses to specific problems that will serve until a better approach is found or conditions change. They're referred to as "countermeasures," rather than "solutions," because that would imply a permanent resolution to a problem. Over the years, the company has developed a robust set of tools and practices that it uses as countermeasures, but many have changed or even been eliminated as improvements are made.

So whether a company does or does not use any particular tool or practice is no indication that it is truly applying Toyota's rules of design and improvement. In particular, contrary to the impression that the concept of zero inventory is at the heart of the Toyota system, we've observed many cases in which Toyota actually built up its inventory of materials as a countermeasure. The ideal system would in fact have no need for inventory. But, in practice, certain circumstances may require it:

- **Unpredictable downtime or yields.** Sometimes a person or a machine is unable to respond on demand when a request is made because of an unexpected mechanical breakdown. For this reason, safety stock is held to protect the customer against random occurrences. The person responsible for ensuring the reliability of a machine or process owns that inventory and strives to reduce the frequency and length of downtimes so that the amount of the safety stock can be reduced.

- **Time-consuming setups.** Difficulties in switching a machine from processing one kind of product to another can prevent a supplier from responding immediately. Therefore, suppliers will produce the product in batch sizes greater than one and hold the excess as inventory so it can respond immediately to the customer. Of course, suppliers will continually try to reduce the changeover time to keep batch sizes and stores of inventory as small as possible. Here, the owners of both the problem and the countermeasure are the machine operator and the team leader, who are responsible for reducing changeover times and batch sizes.

- **Volatility in the mix and volume of customer demand.** In some cases, variations in customers' needs are so large and unpredictable that it is impossible for a plant to adjust its production to them quickly enough. In those instances, buffer stock is kept at or near the shipping point as a countermeasure. The buffer stock also serves as a signal to production and sales managers that the person who works most directly with the customer must help that customer eliminate the underlying causes of any preventable swings in demand.

In many cases, the same type of product is held in different types of inventory. Toyota does not pool its various kinds of inventory, even though doing so would reduce its inventory needs in the short term. That might sound paradoxical for a management system so popularly known to abhor waste. But the paradox can be resolved when we recognize that Toyota's managers and workers are trying to match each countermeasure to each problem.

There's no link between the reason for keeping safety stock—process unreliability—and the reason for keeping buffer stock—fluctuations in customer demand. To pool the two would make it hard to distinguish between the separate activities and customer-supplier connections involved. The inventory would have many owners, and the reasons for its use would become ambiguous. Pooling the inventory thus muddles both the ownership and cause of the problems, making it difficult to introduce improvements.

**Originally published in September–October 1999**
**Reprint 99509**

# Learning to Lead at Toyota

STEVEN J. SPEAR

## Executive Summary

MANY COMPANIES HAVE TRIED to copy Toyota's famous production system—but without success. Why? Part of the reason, says the author, is that imitators fail to recognize the underlying principles of the Toyota Production System (TPS), focusing instead on specific tools and practices.

This article tells the other part of the story. Building on a previous HBR article, "Decoding the DNA of the Toyota Production System," Spear explains how Toyota inculcates managers with TPS principles. He describes the training of a star recruit—a talented young American destined for a high-level position at one of Toyota's U.S. plants. Rich in detail, the story offers four basic lessons for any company wishing to train its managers to apply Toyota's system:

- *There's no substitute for direct observation.* Toyota employees are encouraged to observe failures as they occur—for example, by sitting next to a machine on the assembly line and waiting and watching for any problems.

- *Proposed changes should always be structured as experiments.* Employees embed explicit and testable assumptions in the analysis of their work. That allows them to examine the gaps between predicted and actual results.

- *Workers and managers should experiment as frequently as possible.* The company teaches employees at all levels to achieve continuous improvement through quick, simple experiments rather than through lengthy, complex ones.

- *Managers should coach, not fix.* Toyota managers act as enablers, directing employees but not telling them where to find opportunities for improvements.

Rather than undergo a brief period of cursory walk-throughs, orientations, and introductions as incoming fast-track executives at most companies might, the executive in this story learned TPS the long, hard way—by practicing it, which is how Toyota trains any new employee, regardless of rank or function.

---

TOYOTA IS ONE OF THE world's most storied companies, drawing the attention of journalists, researchers, and executives seeking to benchmark its famous production system. For good reason: Toyota has repeatedly outperformed its competitors in quality, reliability, productivity, cost reduction, sales and market share growth, and market capitalization. By the end of last year it was on the verge of replacing DaimlerChrysler as the third-largest North American car company in terms of production, not just sales. In terms of global market share, it has recently overtaken Ford to become the second-largest carmaker. Its net income and market capitalization by the end of 2003 exceeded those of all its competitors. But those very achievements beg a question: If Toyota has been so widely studied and copied, why have so few companies been able to match its performance?

In our 1999 HBR article, "Decoding the DNA of the Toyota Production System," H. Kent Bowen and I argued that part of the problem is that most outsiders have focused on Toyota's tools and tactics—kanban pull systems, cords, production cells, and the like—and not on its basic set of operating principles. In our article, we identified four such principles, or rules, which together ensure that regular work is tightly coupled with learning how to do the work better. These principles lead to ongoing improvements in reliability, flexibility, safety, and efficiency, and, hence, market share and profitability.

As we explained in the article, Toyota's real achievement is not merely the creation and use of the tools themselves; it is in making all its work a series of nested, ongoing experiments, be the work as routine as installing seats in cars or as complex, idiosyncratic, and large scale as designing and launching a new model or factory. We argued that Toyota's much-noted commitment to standardization is not for the purpose of control or even for capturing a best practice, per se. Rather, standardization—or more precisely, the explicit specification of how work is going to be done *before it is performed*—is coupled with testing work *as it is being done*. The end result is that gaps between what is expected and what actually occurs become immediately evident. Not only are problems contained, prevented from propagating and compromising someone else's work, but the gaps between expectations and reality are investigated; a deeper understanding of the product, process, and people is gained; and that understanding is incorporated into a new specification, which becomes a temporary "best practice" until a new problem is discovered. (See "The Power of Principles" at the end of this article.)

It is one thing to realize that the Toyota Production System (TPS) is a system of nested experiments through which operations are constantly improved. It is another to have an organization in which employees and managers at all levels in all functions are able to live those principles and teach others to apply them. Decoding the DNA of Toyota doesn't mean that you can replicate it.

So how exactly does a company replicate it? In the following pages, I try to answer that question by describing how a talented young American, hired for an upper-level position at one of Toyota's U.S. plants, was initiated into the TPS. His training was hardly what he might have expected given his achievements. With several degrees from top-tier universities, he had already managed large plants for one of Toyota's North American competitors. But rather than undergo a brief period of cursory walk-throughs, orientations, and introductions that an incoming fast-track executive might expect, he learned TPS the long, hard way—by practicing it, which is how Toyota trains any new employee regardless of rank or function. It would take more than three months before he even arrived at the plant in which he was to be a manager.

Our American hotshot, whom we'll call Bob Dallis, arrived at the company thinking that he already knew the basics of TPS—having borrowed ideas from Toyota to improve operations in his previous job—and would simply be fine-tuning his knowledge to improve operations at his new assignment. He came out of his training realizing that improving actual operations was not *his* job—it was the job of the workers themselves. His role was to help them understand that responsibility and enable them to carry it out. His training taught him how to construct work as experiments, which would yield continuous learning and improvements, and to teach others to do the same.

## The Program

Dallis arrived at Toyota's Kentucky headquarters early one wintry morning in January 2002. He was greeted by Mike Takahashi (not his real name), a senior manager of the Toyota Supplier Support Center (TSSC), a group responsible for developing Toyota's and supplier plants' competency in TPS. As such, Takahashi was responsible for Dallis's orientation into the company. Once the introductory formalities had been completed, Takahashi ushered Dallis to his car and proceeded to drive not to the plant where Dallis was to eventually work but to another Toyota engine plant where Dallis would begin his integration into the company. That integration was to involve 12 intensive weeks in the U.S. engine plant and ten days working and making observations in Toyota and Toyota supplier plants in Japan. The content of Dallis's training—as with that of any other Toyota manager—would depend on what, in Takahashi's judgment, Dallis most needed.

### BACK TO BASICS

Bob Dallis's first assignment at the U.S. engine plant was to help a small group of 19 engine-assembly workers

improve labor productivity, operational availability of
machines and equipment, and ergonomic safety.[1] For the
first six weeks, Takahashi engaged Dallis in cycles of
observing and changing individuals' work processes,
thereby focusing on productivity and safety. Working
with the group's leaders, team leaders, and team members, Dallis would document, for instance, how different
tasks were carried out, who did what tasks under what
circumstances, and how information, material, and services were communicated. He would make changes to
try to solve the problems he had observed and then evaluate those changes.

Dallis was not left to his own devices, despite his previous experience and accomplishments. Meetings with
Takahashi bracketed his workweek. On Mondays, Dallis
would explain the following: how he thought the assembly process worked, based on his previous week's observations and experiences; what he thought the line's
problems were; what changes he and the others had
implemented or had in mind to solve those problems;
and the expected impact of his recommendations. On
Fridays, Takahashi reviewed what Dallis had done, com-
paring actual outcomes with the plans and expectations
they had discussed on Monday.

In the first six weeks, 25 changes were implemented
to individual tasks. For instance, a number of parts racks
were reconfigured to present materials to the operators
more comfortably, and a handle on a machine was repo-
sitioned to reduce wrist strain and improve ergonomic
safety. Dallis and the rest of the group also made 75 recommendations for redistributing their work. These were
more substantial changes that required a reconfiguration
of the work area. For instance, changing the place where
a particular part was installed required relocating material stores and moving the light curtains, along with their

attendant wiring and computer coding. These changes were made with the help of technical specialists from the maintenance and engineering departments while the plant was closed over the weekend, after Dallis's fifth week.

Dallis and Takahashi spent Dallis's sixth week studying the group's assembly line to see if the 75 changes actually had the desired effects. They discovered that worker productivity and ergonomic safety had improved significantly, as shown in the exhibit "The U.S. Engine Plant Assembly Line—Before and After." Unfortunately, the changes had also reduced the operational availability of the machines. This is not to say that the changes that improved productivity and ergonomics made the machines malfunction more often. Rather, before the changes were made, there was enough slack in the work so that if a machine faulted, there was often no consequence or inconvenience to anyone. But with Dallis's changes, the group was able to use 15 people instead of 19 to accomplish the same amount of work. It was also able to reduce the time required for each task and improve workload balance. With a much tighter system, previously inconsequential machine problems now had significant effects.

After Dallis had improved the human tasks in the assembly line, Takahashi had him switch to studying how the machines worked. This took another six weeks, with Takahashi and Dallis again meeting on Mondays and Fridays. Takahashi had Dallis, holder of two master's degrees in engineering, watch individual machines until they faulted so that he could investigate causes directly. This took some time. Although work-method failures occurred nearly twice a minute, machine failures were far less frequent and were often hidden inside the machine.

But as Dallis observed the machines and the people working around them, he began to see that a number of failures seemed to be caused by people's interactions with the machines. For instance, Dallis noticed that as one worker loaded gears in a jig that he then put into the machine, he would often inadvertently trip the trigger switch before the jig was fully aligned, causing the apparatus to fault. To solve that problem, Dallis had the maintenance department relocate the switch. Dallis also

---

### The U.S. Engine Plant Assembly Line—Before and After

*The following table describes the impact of the changes Dallis made to the U.S. engine plant assembly line during his first six weeks there. He made substantial improvements in productivity—reducing the number of workers and cycle times. He and the group also made significant improvements in safety (eliminating four processes and improving the rest). But machine availability actually decreased during the period from 90% to 80%. In Dallis's second six weeks, he and his team were able to restore availability back to 90%, but this was still below the 95% target.*

|  | Before | After |
|---|---|---|
| **Productivity** |  |  |
| Number of operators | 19 | 15 |
| Cycle time | 34 seconds | 33 seconds |
| Total work time/engine | 661 seconds | 495 seconds |
| **Ergonomics*** |  |  |
| Red processes | 7 | 1 |
| Yellow processes | 2 | 2 |
| Green processes | 10 | 12 |
| **Operational availability** | ≈90% | ≈80% |

*Processes were rated from worst (red) to best (green) on the basis of their ergonomics—a formula that took into account weight lifted, reaching, twisting, and other risk factors.

observed another operator push a pallet into a machine. After investigating several mechanical failures, he realized that the pallet sometimes rode up onto a bumper in the machine. By replacing the machine's bumper with one that had a different cross-section profile, he was able to eliminate this particular cause of failure. Direct observation of the devices, root-cause analysis of each fault, and immediate reconfiguration to remove suspected causes raised operational availability to 90%, a substantial improvement though still below the 95% target that Takahashi had set for Dallis.

## THE MASTER CLASS

After 12 weeks at the U.S. engine plant, Takahashi judged that Dallis had made progress in observing people and machines and in structuring countermeasures as experiments to be tested. However, Takahashi was concerned that Dallis still took too much of the burden on himself for making changes and that the rate at which he was able to test and refine improvements was too slow. He decided it was time to show Dallis how Toyota practiced improvements on its home turf. He and Dallis flew to Japan, and Dallis's first three days there were spent working at Toyota's famous Kamigo engine plant— where Taiichi Ohno, one of the main architects of TPS, had developed many of his major innovations. On the morning of their arrival, Takahashi unleashed the first of several surprises: Dallis was to work alongside an employee in a production cell and was to make 50 improvements—actual changes in how work was done— during his time there. This worked out to be one change every 22 minutes, not the one per day he had been averaging in his first five weeks of training.

The initial objective set for Dallis was to reduce the "overburden" on the worker—walking, reaching, and other efforts that didn't add value to the product and tired or otherwise impeded the worker and lengthened cycle times. Dallis's workmate could not speak English, and no translator was provided, so the two had to learn to communicate through the physical environment and through models, drawings, and role-playing. Afterward, Dallis speculated that the logic of starting with "overburden" was to get buy-in from the worker who was being asked to do his regular job while being interrupted by a non-Japanese-speaking stranger. There is also semantic significance in the phrasing: Focusing on "overburden" emphasizes the impact of the work design on the person. By contrast, focusing on "waste" suggests that the person is the problem.

Dallis applied the approach he had learned at the U.S. engine plant. On day one, he spent the first three hours observing his new workmate, and by the shift's end proudly reported that he had seven ideas, four of which he and his workmate had implemented. Then Takahashi unleashed his next surprise: He told Dallis that two Japanese team leaders who were going through the same training—people with jobs far less senior than the one for which Dallis was being prepared—had generated 28 and 31 change ideas, respectively, within the same amount of time. Somewhat humbled, Dallis picked up the pace, looking for more opportunities to make improvements and trying even more "quick and dirty" methods of testing ideas: bolting rather than welding things, taping rather than bolting, and holding rather than taping—anything to speed up the rate of feedback. By 11 am on the second day, he and his coworker had built the list to 25 ideas. Takahashi would visit the machine shop while they were working, ask what Dallis was concentrating on, and then follow up with very specific queries about the change idea. "Before I could give a speculative answer," recalled Dallis, "he sent me to look or try for myself."

Dallis found that his ability to identify and resolve problems grew with practice, and by the morning of the third day, he had moved from examining the details of individual work routines to looking at problems with how the production cell as a whole was laid out and the effects on workers' physical movements: "There were two machines, with gauges and parts racks. A tool change took eight steps on one and 24 on the other. Was there a better layout that would reduce the number of steps and time? We figured out how to simulate the change before getting involved with heavy machinery to move the equipment for real," Dallis said. By the time the three days were up, he had identified 50 problems with quality checks, tool changes, and other work in his machine shop—35 of which had been fixed on the spot. (The effects of these changes are summarized in the exhibit "The Kamigo Report Card.")

Takahashi had Dallis conclude his shop-floor training by presenting his work to the plant manager, the machine shop manager, and the shop's group leaders. Along the way, Dallis had been keeping a careful log of the changes and their effects. The log listed operations in the shop, the individual problems Dallis had observed, the countermeasure for each problem, the effect of the change, and the first- and second-shift workers' reactions to the countermeasure. (For a snapshot of the log, see the exhibit "Excerpts from Dallis's Log.") Photographs and diagrams complemented the descriptions. "During the presentations," Dallis reported, "the plant's

## The Kamigo Report Card

*During his three days at Kamigo's machining shop, Dallis documented the effects of the 50 changes he made to work motion (the physical movements of assembly-line workers) and cell layout. The changes are categorized according to the nature of the activity—walking, reaching, or other movements. They cut about half a mile of walking per shift per operator in addition to reducing ergonomic and safety hazards.*

| | QUALITY CHECKS* | | | TOOL CHANGES* | | | OTHER WORK |
|---|---|---|---|---|---|---|---|
| | **Walking** | **Reaching** | **Other** | **Walking** | **Reaching** | **Other** | |
| **Number of changes** | 8 | 8 | 13 | 7 | 4 | 5 | 5 |
| **Effect of changes** | 20-meter reduction (50%) per check | 2-meter reduction in reaching | Elimination of tripping risk, organization of tools to reduce risk of confusion | 50-meter reduction per tool change | 180-cm reduction in reaching | Improvement of ergonomics, organization to reduce risk of confusion | Elimination of tripping risk, simplification of oil change |

*Quality checks were performed two to three times an hour, and tool changes were made once an hour.

## Excerpts from Dallis's Log

Throughout his training, Dallis kept a precise log of identified problems, proposed solutions, expected results, and actual outcomes. Records like the one below are essential to the Toyota Production System, as they help encourage the precision that is necessary for true experimentation.

The following excerpt shows two of the problems Dallis identified. Note that he obtained approval of his changes from the people actually doing the work. That's because at the end of the day, the people doing the work must own the solution. This kind of hierarchical inversion is a common feature of Toyota operations.

| Problem # | Location | Description | Countermeasure | Result | Date | Shift 1 approval | Shift 2 approval |
|---|---|---|---|---|---|---|---|
| 4 | Station 6R | Team member walks 4 meters to get and then return first-piece check gauge during tool changes | Move first-piece check gauge from table to shelf between stations 5 and 6 | 4-meter reduction in walk/tool change | May 8 | Yes | Yes |
| 58 | Part gauging area | Team member walks 5 steps to return cams to return chute, walking around light pole | Remove light pole (obstruction) and move part gauge 45° | Reduce walk 2 steps | Not done | Yes (Pending help from maintenance department) | Yes |

general manager, the machine shop's manager, and its group leaders were engaged in what [I and the other] 'lowly' team leaders said. Two-thirds [of the audience] actively took notes during the team leaders' presentations, asking pointed questions throughout."

After Dallis made his presentation, Takahashi spent the remaining week showing him how Toyota group leaders—people responsible for a few assembly or machining teams, each with three to seven members—managed and presented their improvement projects. In one case, a group leader was exploring ways of reducing machine changeover times and establishing a more even production pace for an injection-molding process. In another, a group leader was looking for ways to reduce downtime in a machining operation. In all the presentations, the group leaders explained the problems they were addressing, the processes they used to develop countermeasures, and the effect these countermeasures had on performance. Dallis quickly realized that people at all levels, even those subordinate to the one for which he was being developed, were expected to structure work and improvements as experiments.

## Lessons Learned

Although Takahashi at no point told Dallis exactly what he was supposed to learn from his experience, the methodology of the training just described is so consistent and specific that it reveals at least four fundamental principles underlying the system. Together with the rules we described in our 1999 article, the following lessons may help explain why Toyota has remained the world's preeminent manufacturer.

***Lesson 1   There's no substitute for direct observation.***
Throughout Dallis's training, he was required to watch
employees work and machines operate. He was asked
not to "figure out" why a machine had failed, as if he
were a detective solving a crime already committed, but
to sit and wait until he could directly observe its failure—to wait for it to tell him what he needed to know.

One of the group leader presentations at Kamigo
described this principle in action. In a project to improve
machine maintenance, it became clear to the group that
machine problems were evident only when failures
occurred. In response, the shop's group leaders had
removed opaque covers from several machines so that
operators and team leaders could hear and see the inner
workings of the devices, thus improving their ability to
assess and anticipate problems with the machines. This
is a very different approach from the indirect observation on which most companies rely—reports, interviews,
surveys, narratives, aggregate data, and statistics. Not
that these indirect approaches are wrong or useless.
They have their own value, and there may be a loss of
perspective (the big picture) when one relies solely on
direct observation. But direct observation is essential,
and no combination of indirect methods, however clever,
can possibly take its place.

Dallis's previous experience managing plants might
have prepared him to look at operations of greater scale
and scope, but had Takahashi given him a project with
greater scope, Dallas might not have learned to observe
with such precision. Dallis's first six weeks at the U.S.
engine plant meant that he had up to 23,824 opportunities to observe complete work cycles. Because his work
was limited to a 19-person line, he could view more than

a thousand work cycles per person. That gave him deep
insight into the line's productivity and safety.

***Lesson 2  Proposed changes should always be struc-
tured as experiments.***  In the scientific method, experiments are used to test a hypothesis, and the results are
used to refine or reject the hypothesis. Dallis's problem
solving was structured so that he embedded explicit
and testable assumptions in his analysis of the work.
Throughout his training, therefore, he had to explain
gaps between predicted and actual results. In his meetings with Takahashi at the U.S. engine plant, for example, he was required to propose hypotheses on Monday
and the results of his experiments on Friday. In Japan, he
had to present his changes as tests of causal relationships, stating the problem he saw, the root cause he suspected, the change he had made, and the countermeasure's actual effect on performance.

Of course, many people trying to improve a process
have some idea of what the problems are and how to fix
them. The difference with TPS—and this is key—is that
it seeks to fully understand both the problem and the
solution. For example, any manager might say, "Maybe
the parts rack should be closer to the assembler's hand. If
we move it here, I'll bet it'll shave a few seconds off the
cycle." Were he to try this and find that it saved six seconds, he would probably be quite pleased and consider
the problem solved.

But in the eyes of a Toyota manager like Takahashi,
such a result would indicate that the manager didn't
fully understand the work that he was trying to improve.
Why hadn't he been more specific about how far he was
going to move the rack? And how many seconds did he
*expect* to save? Four? If the actual savings is six seconds,

that's cause for celebration—but also for additional inquiry. Why was there a two-second difference? With the explicit precision encouraged by Takahashi, the discrepancy would prompt a deeper investigation into how a process worked and, perhaps more important, how a particular person studied and improved the process.

***Lesson 3  Workers and managers should experiment as frequently as possible.***  At Toyota, the focus is on many quick, simple experiments rather than on a few lengthy, complex ones. This became particularly evident when Dallis went to Japan. Whereas in the United States he made 25 changes in six weeks (before the weekend blitz during which 75 were completed), in Japan he had to make 50 changes in 2 shifts, which meant an average of one change every 22 minutes. This encouraged Dallis to learn from making small incremental changes rather than large system-design changes. He would observe work actually being done, quickly see where struggles were occurring, then rapidly test his understanding by implementing a countermeasure, thereby accelerating the rate at which he discovered "contingencies" or "interferences" in the process. This is precisely the way Toyota workers practice process improvement. They cannot "practice" making a change, because a change can be made only once. But they can practice the process of observing and testing many times.

To ensure that Dallis received the practice he needed and that he internalized his understanding of it, Takahashi structured Dallis's training so that the complexity of his experiments increased gradually. When Dallis started at the U.S. engine plant, he conducted "single factor" experiments, changing small, individual work elements rather than taking a system perspective. What's more, his efforts there started with individual work methods, progressing to more complex and subtle machine problems only when he had developed his observation and problem-solving skills over the six weeks. Thus, he moved from problems that were easier to observe to those that were harder. If each learning cycle is kept small and bounded, then the learner can make mistakes and the consequences will not be severe. This approach increases the learner's willingness to take risks and learn by doing. Dallis's training at Kamigo mirrored this progression: He began, once again, with work-method issues of "overburden" before moving on to machines.[2]

*Lesson 4  Managers should coach, not fix.*  Dallis's training not only gave him insight into how Toyota delivers continuous improvement but also helped him understand the unique relationships between Toyota's managers and workers. Dallis himself had been rewarded by his previous employer for being a problem solver, albeit one with a more participative and inclusive approach than most. What he saw at Toyota, by contrast, was workers and low-level managers constantly solving problems. Indeed, the more senior the manager, the less likely he was to be solving problems himself.

Toyota managers act as enablers. Throughout Dallis's training, Takahashi—one of Toyota's most senior operational managers—positioned himself as a teacher and coach, not as a technological specialist. He put Dallis through experiences without explicitly stating what or how he was to learn. Even when specific skills were imparted, these were purely to assist Dallis's observation and experimentation. For instance, Takahashi showed

Dallis how to observe an individual worker in order to
spot instances of stress, wasted effort, and so on, and he
explicitly advised Dallis on how to develop prototypes.
But at no point did he suggest actual process improvements. Rather, he directed Dallis on how to find opportunities for those improvements (as in, study this person
or that machine, looking for various types of stress,
strain, or faults) and on how to develop and test possible
countermeasures.

Takahashi also gave Dallis the resources he needed to
act quickly. For example, at Kamigo, Dallis had the help
of a maintenance worker to move equipment, create fix-
tures, relocate wires and pipes, and provide other skilled
trade work so that he could test as many ideas as possible. Takahashi and the shop manager also came to the
cell of the machining operation to review Dallis's ideas;
they gave him tips on piloting his changes before asking
support workers to make parts or relocate equipment.
When Dallis wanted to rotate some gauges that tested
parts, the shop manager showed him how to quickly and
inexpensively make cardboard prototypes to test location, orientation, size, and so on.

The result of this unusual manager–worker relationship is a high degree of sophisticated problem solving at
all levels of the organization. Dallis noted, "As a former
engine-plant person, I saw a line [at Kamigo] that was 15
years old but that had the capacity to build 90 different
engine types. It was amazing that they solved so many
problems with such simple equipment. Behind the
changes was some pretty deep thinking." The basic company philosophy is that any operating system can be
improved if enough people at every level are looking and
experimenting closely enough. (After all, if only the big

shots were expected to make changes, all that "little" stuff would get overlooked.) The fact that Dallis, after just three months at the U.S. engine plant, was able to empower others to implement 50 improvements at Kamigo, one of Toyota's top plants, offers insight into why Toyota stays ahead of its competitors.[3]

## Back to America

To see if Dallis had learned the right lessons from his training, Takahashi sent him back to the U.S. engine plant where his instruction had begun. As we have seen, Dallis had already helped make substantial improvements in the assembly line's labor productivity and ergonomic safety before going to Japan. But he hadn't been able to raise operational availability to 95%. Now, upon Dallis's return to that plant, Takahashi had him attempt this goal again. However, there was a marked departure from Dallis's earlier approach, in which he primarily saw himself as a problem solver.

With Takahashi's help, Dallis worked with the line's group leader and assistant manager in order to develop the problem-solving skills of the line's team members and team leaders. The point was for the team to learn to solve little problems simultaneously so that the line could recover quickly when problems occurred. For instance, the team realized that it had difficulties in keeping track of what work needed to be done and in identifying problems as they occurred. It therefore had to improve its "visual management" of the work—what was going well, what was going wrong, and what needed to be done. Dallis sat down with the group leader and assistant manager and set out a schedule for identifying specific

problems and allocating responsibility for them across
the team. As the team members observed and developed
countermeasures, Dallis would drop by much as Takahashi had done, asking them specific questions that
would oblige them to observe their allotted problems
more closely as they happened. To its delight, the group
hit its mark ahead of schedule and raised operational
availability to 99%.

Dallis had returned to America with an altered focus.
He had realized from the way Takahashi had managed
his training, and from what he'd seen of others' training,
that the efforts of a senior manager like himself should
be aimed not at making direct improvements but at producing a cadre of excellent group leaders who learn
through continuous experimentation. The target of 95%
operational availability at the U.S. engine plant was the
same, but he now knew whose target it really was, and it
wasn't his. At this point, Takahashi finally released Dallis
from his training to take on his full-time managerial
responsibilities.

For anyone trying to understand how the
Toyota Production System really works, there is probably
no substitute for the kind of total immersion that Dallis
received. TPS is a system you have to live to fully understand, let alone improve. Besides, anyone like Dallis coming into Toyota from the outside, regardless of his or her
experience, is coming into an organization with a long
history of making improvements and modifications at a
pace few organizations have ever approached. No one
can expect to assimilate—let alone recreate—such a
strong and distinct culture in just a few weeks or even a

few months. Nevertheless, any company that develops and implements a training program such as the one Dallis participated in is sure to reap enormous dividends. The organization that applies the rules in designing its operations and that trains its managers to apply those rules will have made a good start at replicating the DNA of the Toyota Production System.

## Notes

1. Operational availability equals machine run time/machine use time. For instance, if a machine requires eight minutes of process time to grind a surface, but, because of jams and other interruptions, ten minutes are actually spent from start to finish, then operational availability would be 80%. Ideally, operationally availability would be 100%—that is, the machine always runs when it is needed.

2. The incremental approach was also helpful to Takahashi, who used it to teach Dallis. He directly observed Dallis's work by creating short learning cycles with rapid feedback so that he could continually reassess Dallis's knowledge and skills, both to provide feedback in order to help him learn and to design the next learning increment.

3. According to Takahashi, the expectation was that group leaders at Kamigo—managers who supervised several operating shops or cells—would spend 70% of their time doing process improvement work. This time would often be shared among three to four teams, implying that team leaders—people managing one shop or cell—were expected to spend a minimum of 20% of their time on improvement work.

# The Power of Principles

THE INSIGHT THAT Toyota applies underlying principles rather than specific tools and processes explains why the company continues to outperform its competitors. Many companies have tried to imitate Toyota's tools as opposed to its principles; as a result, many have ended up with rigid, inflexible production systems that worked well in the short term but didn't stand the test of time.

Recognizing that TPS is about applying principles rather than tools enables companies that in no way resemble Toyota to tap into its sources of success. Alcoa, a company whose large-scale processes—refining, smelting, and so on—bear little resemblance to Toyota's discrete-parts fabrication and assembly operations, has based its Alcoa Business System (ABS) on the TPS rules. Alcoa claims that ABS saved the company $1.1 billion from 1998 to 2000, while improving safety, productivity, and quality.

In another example, pilot projects applying the rules at the University of Pittsburgh Medical Center and other health care organizations have led to huge improvements in medication administration, nursing, and other critical processes, delivering better quality care to patients, relieving workers of nonproductive burdens, as well as providing costs savings and operating efficiencies.

**Originally published in May 2004**
**Reprint R0405E**

# Aligning Incentives in Supply Chains

V.G. NARAYANAN AND ANANTH RAMAN

## Executive Summary

MOST COMPANIES DON'T WORRY about the behavior of their supply chain partners. Instead, they expect the supply chain to work efficiently without interference, as if guided by Adam Smith's famed invisible hand. In their study of more than 50 supply networks, V.G. Narayanan and Ananth Raman found that companies often looked out for their own interests and ignored those of their network partners. Consequently, supply chains performed poorly.

Those results aren't shocking when you consider that supply chains extend across several functions and many companies, each with its own priorities and goals. Yet all those functions and firms must pull in the same direction for a chain to deliver goods and services to consumers quickly and cost-effectively.

According to the authors, a supply chain works well only if the risks, costs, and rewards of doing business are distributed fairly across the network. In fact, misaligned incentives are often the cause of excess inventory, stock-outs, incorrect forecasts, inadequate sales efforts, and even poor customer service. The fates of all supply chain partners are interlinked: If the firms work together to serve consumers, they will all win. However, they can do that only if incentives are aligned.

Companies must acknowledge that the problem of incentive misalignment exists and then determine its root cause and align or redesign incentives. They can improve alignment by, for instance, adopting revenue-sharing contracts, using technology to track previously hidden information, or working with intermediaries to build trust among network partners. It's also important to periodically reassess incentives, because even top-performing networks find that changes in technology or business conditions alter the alignment of incentives.

---

W ALL STREET STILL REMEMBERS the day it heard that Cisco's much-vaunted supply chain had snapped. On a mad Monday, April 16, 2001, the world's largest network-equipment maker shocked investors when it warned them that it would soon scrap around $2.5 billion of surplus raw materials—one of the largest inventory write-offs in U.S. business history. The company reported in May a net loss of $2.69 billion for the quarter, and its share price tumbled by approximately 6% on the day it made that announcement. Cisco was perhaps blind-sided by the speed with which the United States had advanced into recession, but how could this paragon of supply chain management have misread demand by $2.5 billion, almost half as much as its sales in the quarter? Experts blamed the company's new forecasting software, and analysts accused senior executives of burying their heads in sockets, but those experts and analysts were mostly wrong.

In truth, Cisco ended up with a mountain of sub-assembly boards and semiconductors it didn't need because of the way its supply chain partners had behaved in the previous 18 months. Cisco doesn't have production facilities, so it passes orders to contract manufacturers. The contractors had stockpiled semifinished products because demand for Cisco's products usually exceeded supply. They had an incentive to build buffer stocks: Cisco rewarded them when they delivered supplies quickly. Many contractors also boosted their profit margins by buying large volumes from component suppliers at lower prices than Cisco had negotiated. Since the contractors and component makers had everything to gain and nothing to lose by building excess inventory, they worked overtime to do so without worrying about Cisco's real needs.

When demand slowed in the first half of fiscal 2000, Cisco found that it couldn't cut off supplies quickly. Moreover, it wasn't clear what Cisco had asked its suppliers to produce and what the contractors had manufactured in anticipation of Cisco's orders. Many contractors believed that Cisco had implicitly assured them it would buy everything they could produce. Since Cisco hadn't stipulated the responsibilities and accountability of its contractors and component suppliers, much of the excess inventory ended up in its warehouses. However, the supply chain imploded because Cisco's partners acted in ways that weren't in the best interests of the company or the supply chain.

It's tempting to ask, in retrospect, "What *was* everyone thinking?" But Cisco's supply chain is the rule rather than an exception. Most companies don't worry about the behavior of their partners while building supply chains to deliver goods and services to consumers. Engineers—not psychologists—build supply networks. Every firm behaves in ways that maximize its own interests, but companies assume, wrongly, that when they do so, they also maximize the supply chain's interests. In this mistaken view, the quest for individual benefit leads to collective good, as Adam Smith argued about markets more than two centuries ago. Supply chains are expected to work efficiently without interference, as if guided by Smith's invisible hand. But our research over the last ten years shows that executives have assumed too much. We found, in more than 50 supply chains we studied, that companies often didn't act in ways that maximized the network's profits; consequently, the supply chains performed poorly.

That finding isn't shocking when you consider that supply chains extend across several functions and many companies, each of which has its own priorities and goals. Yet all those functions and firms must pull in the same direction to ensure that supply chains deliver goods and services quickly and cost-effectively. Executives tackle intraorganizational problems but overlook cross-company problems because the latter are difficult to detect. They also find it tedious and time-consuming to define roles, responsibilities, and accountability for a string of businesses they don't manage directly. Besides, coordinating actions across firms is tough because organizations have different cultures and companies can't count on shared beliefs or loyalty to motivate their partners. To induce supply chain partners to behave in ways that are best for everybody, companies have to create or modify monetary incentives.

A supply chain works well if its companies' incentives are aligned—that is, if the risks, costs, and rewards of doing business are distributed fairly across the network. For reasons that we shall later discuss, if incentives aren't in line, the companies' actions won't optimize the chain's performance. Indeed, misaligned incentives are often the cause of excess inventory, stock-outs, incorrect forecasts, inadequate sales efforts, and even poor customer service.

When incentives aren't aligned in supply chains, it's not just operational efficiency that's at stake. In recent years, many companies have assumed that supply costs are more or less fixed and have fought with suppliers for a bigger share of the pie. For instance, U.S. automobile manufacturers have antagonized their vendors by demanding automatic price reductions every year. Our research, however, shows that a company can increase the size of the pie itself by aligning partners' incentives. Thus, the fates of all supply chain members are interlinked: If the companies work together to efficiently deliver goods and services to consumers, they will all win. If they don't, they will all lose to another supply chain. The challenge is to get all the firms in your supply network to play the game so that everybody wins. The only way you can do that is by aligning incentives.

## Why Incentives Get out of Line

Companies often complain to us that their supply chain partners don't seem to want to do what is in everyone's best interests, even when it's obvious what's best for the supply chain. This obstructive attitude, we believe, is a telltale sign that incentives have gotten out of line and companies are chasing different goals.

There are three reasons why incentive-related issues arise in supply chains. First, when companies cannot observe other firms' actions, they find it hard to persuade those firms to do their best for the supply network. A simple illustration: Whirlpool relies on retailers like Sears to sell its washing machines because retailers' salespeople greatly influence consumer decisions. If Whirlpool doesn't offer lucrative margins on its products, Sears will plug products that do or will encourage shoppers to buy its private-label brand, Kenmore. However, Whirlpool can't observe or track the effort that Sears expends in pushing its products. Since Sears's actions are hidden from Whirlpool, the manufacturer finds it tough to create incentives that induce the retailer to do what's best for both companies. Such "hidden actions," as we call them, exist all along the supply chain.

Second, it's difficult to align interests when one company has information or knowledge that others in the supply chain don't. For example, most U.S. automotive vendors fear that if they share their cost data, the Big Three auto manufacturers will use that information to squeeze the vendors' margins. For that reason, suppliers are reluctant to participate in improvement initiatives that would let manufacturers or other companies collect such data. Since the suppliers insist on hiding information, the Big Three's supply chains don't function as efficiently as they could.

Third, incentive schemes are often badly designed. Our favorite example of this problem is a Canadian bread manufacturer that felt it needed to increase its stocks in stores. The manufacturer allotted deliverymen a certain amount of its shelf space in stores and offered them commissions based on sales off those shelves. The deliverymen gladly kept the store shelves filled—even on days when rival bread makers were offering consumers deep discounts on their products. The Canadian baker had to throw away heaps of stale loaves, and its costs soared as a result. The deliverymen earned handsome commissions, but the company's profits fell because of an ill-conceived incentive scheme.

## Straightening Things Out

Our research suggests that companies must align incentives in three stages. At the outset, executives need to acknowledge that there's misalignment. Then they must trace the problem to hidden actions, hidden information, or badly designed incentives. Finally, by using one of three approaches that we describe in detail later in the article, companies can align or redesign incentives to obtain the behavior they desire from their partners.

### ACCEPT THE PREMISE

When we conduct straw polls with executives, almost all of them admit they hadn't thought that incentive alignment was a problem in their supply chains. We're not surprised. Most companies find it difficult at first to come to grips with the relationship between incentives and supply chain problems. Executives don't understand the operational details of other firms well enough to realize that incentives could be getting out of whack. In addition, companies tend to avoid the subject of monetary incentives because, if they raise it, their partners may suspect them of merely trying to negotiate lower prices for the products or services they buy.

Once companies get past these mental barriers, it's relatively easy for them to detect incentive misalignment. They should expect problems to surface whenever they launch change initiatives, because these modify the incentives of key stakeholders—and most stakeholders protest loudly when incentives get out of line. For instance, in the late 1990s, businesses ranging from Campbell Soup to Liz Claiborne fought the bullwhip effect—amplified fluctuations in demand—by managing inventory themselves. Rather than relying on distributors and retailers for orders, the companies set up central logistics departments to make purchasing decisions. Although these initiatives could have helped the companies' supply chains, they failed because of open resistance from distributors and retailers, who were convinced that the manufacturers had marginalized their roles.

## PINPOINT THE CAUSE

Executives must get to the root of incentive problems, so they can choose the best approach to bring incentives back into line. In our consulting work with companies, we often use role play for this purpose. We ask senior managers to identify decisions that would have been made differently if they or their suppliers had focused on the supply chain's interests instead of their own interests. We then ask why decision makers acted as they did. In some cases, the answers suggest improper training or inadequate decision-support tools for managers; most of the time, however, they point to mismatched goals. And we try to figure out whether the decisions were motivated by hidden actions, hidden information, or badly designed incentives.

Aligning incentives is quite unlike other supply chain challenges, which are amenable to structured problem-solving processes that involve equations and algorithms. In our experience, only managers who understand the motivations of most companies in their supply chain can tackle incentive-related issues. Since alignment also requires an understanding of functions such as marketing, manufacturing, logistics, and finance, it's essential to involve senior managers in the process.

## ALIGN OR REDESIGN

Once companies have identified the root causes of incentive problems, they can use one of three types of solutions—contract based, information based, or trust based—to bring incentives back into line. Most organizations don't have the influence to redesign an entire chain's incentives—they can change only the incentives of their immediate partners. While it is often the biggest company in the supply chain that aligns incentives, size is neither necessary nor sufficient for the purpose. In the late 1980s, the $136 million Swedish company Kanthal, a supplier of heating wires, said that it would impose penalties whenever the $35 billion GE changed specifications without warning. The mighty GE agreed to contract changes requested by its small partner, and incentives became better aligned as a result.

# Rewriting Contracts

One way companies can align incentives in supply chains is by altering contracts with partner firms. When misalignment stems from hidden actions, executives can bring those actions to the surface—unhide them, as it were—by creating a contract that rewards or penalizes partners based on outcomes. To return to an earlier example, Whirlpool may not be able to see what Sears's salespeople do to promote the manufacturer's washing machines, but it can track the outcome of their efforts— namely, increased or decreased sales—and draw up agreements to reward them accordingly.

It's necessary to alter contracts when badly designed incentives are the problem. Let us think back to the Canadian bread manufacturer whose deliverymen over-stocked stores when they were paid sales-based commissions. The company changed the deliverymen's behavior by altering their contracts to include penalties for stale loaves in stores, which could be tracked. While the penalties reduced the incentive to overstock stores, the commissions ensured that the deliverymen still kept shelves well stocked.

That may appear to be a minor change, but it's a significant one. Companies often underestimate the power of redesigning contracts. Small changes in incentives can transform supply chains, and they can do so quickly. Take the case of Tweeter, a consumer-electronics retail chain that in May 1996 acquired the loss-making retailer Bryn Mawr Stereo and Video. For years, Bryn Mawr's stores had reported lower sales than rivals had. Tweeter's executives realized early that the incentives that Bryn Mawr offered its store managers would not lead to higher sales. For instance, while Tweeter penalized managers for a small part of the cost of products pilfered from their stores, Bryn Mawr deducted the full value of stolen goods from their pay. Since store managers faced more pressure to prevent shoplifting than to push sales, they behaved accordingly. They placed impulse-purchase products like audiotapes and batteries behind locked cases, which reduced theft but killed sales. They spent more time tracking merchandise receipts than they did showing products to consumers. They shut down stores while receiving merchandise to ensure there was no loss in inventory; never mind the sales they lost in the process.

After the acquisition, Tweeter stopped deducting retail shrink from Bryn Mawr store managers' salaries and started paying them a percentage of the profits from their stores. While both sales and shrink affect profits, the retailer effectively increased the importance of sales relative to shrink. The store managers therefore directed their efforts toward increasing sales rather than decreasing shrink. Although Tweeter left the store name unchanged, kept the product mix intact, and retained the same store managers, Bryn Mawr's sales rose by an average of 10% in 1997. As managers moved merchandise to shelves where consumers could touch products, shrink also increased, from $122 a month to $600 a month per store. Net-net, however, Bryn Mawr's profits rose by 2.5% of sales in those 12 months. Tweeter didn't have to change people to create a new culture at Bryn Mawr; it just changed their incentives. (For more details, see Nicole DeHoratius and Ananth Raman's "Impact of Store Manager Incentives on Retail Performance," a Harvard Business School Working Paper, September 2000.)

By changing how, rather than how much, they pay partners, companies can improve supply chain performance. When that happens, all the firms in the chain make more money than they used to. (See "The Economics of Incentive Alignment" at the end of this article.) In the 1990s, Hollywood movie studios, such as

Universal Studios and Sony Pictures, found that frequent
stock-outs at video retailers, like Blockbuster and Movie
Gallery, posed a major problem. A lack of inventory on
store shelves meant that everyone suffered: The studios
lost potential sales, video rental companies lost income,
and consumers went home disgusted. Inventory levels
were low because the incentives of the studios and the
retailers weren't in line. The studios sold retailers copies
of movies at $60 a videotape. At an average rental of $3,
the retailers had to ensure that each tape went out at
least 20 times to break even. The studios wanted to sell
more tapes, but the retailers wished to buy fewer tapes
and rent them out more often.

When the studios and the retailers explored the possibility of sharing revenues, incentives began to tee up.
Since it cost the studios only $3 to create a copy of a
movie, they could recoup their investment the first time
a consumer rented a tape. In theory, that meant the studios could stock many more copies than the retailers
could. For the model to work, though, the studios needed
to derive income not from tape sales but from rentals—
as the retailers did.

In the late 1990s, when video rental companies proposed revenue-sharing contracts, the studios raised no
objections. They agreed to sell tapes to the retailers for
around $3 per tape and receive 50% of the revenues from
each rental. However, the studios needed to track the
retailers' revenues and inventories for the revenue-
sharing system to work. The studios and the video rental
companies relied on an intermediary, Rentrak, which
obtained data from the retailers' computerized records
and conducted store audits to ensure that all tapes were
accounted for. In fact, the contract-based solution

wouldn't have worked if Rentrak hadn't revealed previously hidden information in the supply chain.

In less than a year, it became clear that revenue sharing had led to a happy ending in the video rental industry. The studios saw a bounce in their bottom lines, retailers began to earn more money, and consumers no longer went away disappointed. Industry experts estimated that rental revenues from videotapes increased by 15% in the United States, and the studios and the retailers enjoyed a 5% growth in profits. Perhaps most important, stock-outs at video rental stores fell from 25% before revenue sharing to less than 5% after revenue sharing.

## Revealing Hidden Information

Companies can also align incentives across the supply chain by tracking and monitoring more business variables, thereby making actions visible, or by disseminating information throughout the supply chain.

The most effective way to reveal hidden actions is to measure more variables. In the late 1980s, Campbell Soup offered distributors discounts several times every year, hoping that the savings would be passed on to retailers. However, distributors bought more units than they sold to retailers, so Campbell's sales fluctuated wildly. For instance, the company sold 40% of its chicken noodle soup each of those years during six-week promotional periods. The uptick put a lot of pressure on the company's supply chain. When Campbell realized that it gathered data on distributors' purchases but not on their sales, it invested in information technology systems that could track both. Then, by giving the distributors

discounts on sales but not on purchases, Campbell eliminated the incentive to forward-buy large quantities. That
helped improve the supply chain's performance.

Technology isn't always needed for managers to
observe more variables. Some companies employ mystery shoppers—agents who pose as customers—to ascer-
tain whether, say, distributors are pushing products or
retailers are offering services. Like many franchisers,
Mobil uses mystery shoppers to monitor restroom clean-
liness and employee friendliness at its gas stations.

Information systems derived from the principles of
activity-based costing are critical for measuring the costs
associated with hidden actions. No company knows that
better than Owens & Minor, a large distributor of medical supplies. Hospitals used to pay O&M a fixed percentage of the cost of items delivered. They could, however,
buy supplies directly from manufacturers if it was
cheaper to do so. For example, the hospitals sometimes
bought high-margin products such as cardiovascular
sutures from manufacturers to avoid the distributor's
markup. The hospitals expected O&M to supply products with high storage, handling, and transportation
costs—adult diapers, for instance—even though those
items gave the distributor low margins. Cost-plus contracts led to a misalignment in another area, too: In general, distributors were often reluctant to provide services
such as just-in-time deliveries, while the hospitals
demanded more such services for the same fixed
markup.

O&M found an opportunity to realign incentives
when it switched to an activity-based costing system
and got a handle on the profitability of its services to
hospitals. Until then, O&M knew when its customers
requested services such as emergency deliveries; what it

didn't know was the effect of those requests on its costs and profits. In other words, customers' actions weren't hidden from O&M, but the impact of those actions was. After O&M had figured out the cost of its services, the distributor asked customers for fees according to the services they desired. But first, to test the change, O&M approached a hospital that had rejected its overtures two years earlier. O&M explained that instead of offering a cost-plus contract, it would charge per service requested. It shared its cost data with the hospital to show that the fees weren't unreasonable.

The hospital's reaction was so encouraging that, in 1996, O&M offered all its customers a choice between an activity-based-pricing system and a traditional contract. O&M's activity-based contracts offered hospitals a menu of services and quoted a price for each one. A hospital could choose just-in-time deliveries, for example, but it would have to pay for them. O&M believed that by designing mutually beneficial incentives, it could induce hospitals to act in ways that would be good for both themselves and O&M. The company wasn't wrong; most hospitals were happy to have a distributor provide all the services they wanted, even if that meant paying extra. In 2003, O&M's sales from activity-based-pricing contracts reached $1.35 billion, which was nearly one-third of its turnover of $4.2 billion.

## Developing Trust

Companies can sometimes use trust-based mechanisms to prevent incentive problems from cropping up in supply chains. That may sound like a contradiction, since firms are more likely to trust each other when their incentives are in line. When companies realize from the

outset that working with partners will not be easy,
though, they can use intermediaries to prevent supply
chains from breaking down. The use of a middleman has
become more popular as American and European companies have outsourced manufacturing to developing
countries, where legal contracts are often harder to
enforce.

When Western companies link up with Asian manufacturers or component suppliers, each party has misgivings about the other's interests. The importers are convinced that the vendors won't deliver on time, can't
produce consistent quality, and will give greater priority
to companies that will pay higher prices. They also fear
that the contractors will reduce their costs by bribing
government officials or using child labor. As Nike found,
those dubious practices give importers, rather than their
suppliers, bad reputations. For their part, suppliers fear
that importers might reject products. Since importers
enter into contracts six to nine months in advance of
delivery, vendors doubt companies' ability to predict
consumer demand accurately. They worry that demand
for products will be lower than anticipated and that
importers will reject consignments, pretending that the
quality wasn't up to snuff.

Under those circumstances, the presence of an intermediary can help align the incentives of the two parties.
For instance, the Hong Kong–based supply chain intermediary Li & Fung has become adept at marrying the
interests of manufacturers and suppliers. The company,
which has created a network of factories in Asia,
enforces a code of ethics that precludes its network from
providing unhygienic work conditions, for example, or
paying below the minimum wage. Li & Fung monitors its
suppliers to ensure that they adhere to the quality and

ethical standards that Western importers demand. It employs a chief compliance officer, who reports directly to the company's chairperson. Li & Fung accounts for roughly half the volumes of all its suppliers every year. If a vendor reneges on its promises, it stands to lose a great deal of business from Li & Fung. At the same time, Li & Fung keeps multinational companies honest. If they make frivolous demands of suppliers or refuse to take delivery of products at contracted prices, Li & Fung will deny them access to its network in the future. Thus, Li & Fung is able to align incentives because of the repeat business it offers importers and suppliers.

Just as Li & Fung's reputation reduces the need for formal contracts, so can the relationships between individuals in companies. Klaus Obermeyer, the founder of the fashion skiwear manufacturer Sport Obermeyer, formed a joint venture with the Hong Kong–based supplier Raymond Tse in 1985 to source raw materials, cut and sew garments, and coordinate shipping. Over the last 19 years, Klaus Obermeyer has left most production and investment decisions to Tse. He values his relationship with Tse and, given their history working together, believes that Tse will not make decisions that aren't in both companies' interests. The desire to preserve their relationship has been a sufficient incentive for Obermeyer and Tse to act only in ways that are mutually beneficial.

COMPANIES SHOULD EXPLORE contract-based solutions before they turn to other approaches, because contracts are quick and easy to implement. They should bear in mind, though, that advances in technology have reduced the cost of information-based solutions. For instance, some organizations have made real-time sales data available throughout supply chains—and that was unimaginable five years ago. In fact, we recommend information-based solutions ahead of trust-based ones. Companies can adopt the latter only if they are able to identify trustworthy intermediaries, and that is often difficult.

Before we conclude, we must mention two caveats. First, a solution that resolves incentive misalignment for one company might exacerbate the problem for another. Executives should therefore coordinate the interests of all the companies in a supply chain at the same time. Second, companies must align the incentives of all the key decision makers in their supply chains. Although it is difficult for one company to change the incentives of executives in other organizations, it can point out possible misalignments to partners. Consider the following example: A Boston-based start-up placed kiosks for dispensing its products in retail stores. It offered incentives to retailers but failed to ensure that the retailers passed on those incentives to store managers. Since the store managers could decide where to place the kiosks but weren't motivated to display them prominently, the start-up found kiosks in corners where few consumers would notice them. By flagging the issue for the retailers, the start-up was able to tackle the problem before it got to be too late.

Companies should periodically study their supply chains, because even top-performing networks find that changes in technology or business conditions may alter the alignment of incentives. Firms can take three steps to facilitate discussions about misalignments. First, executives should conduct incentive audits whenever they adopt new technologies or enter new markets. Such audits verify that the incentives offered to key individuals and stakeholders are consistent with the behavior that companies expect of their partners. Second, companies should educate managers about their supply chain partners. Only then will manufacturers better understand distributors, for instance, or will retailers realize the constraints manufacturers face. Third, since executives are often uncomfortable discussing how incentives influence their decisions, it's useful to depersonalize the situation by getting managers to examine case studies from other industries. It's critical to get the conversation started—in most supply chains, having companies admit that incentive problems even exist is more than half the battle.

## A Step-by-Step Approach

COMPANIES FACE INCENTIVE problems in their supply chains because of

- hidden actions by partner firms.
- hidden information—data or knowledge that only some of the firms in the supply chain possess.
- badly designed incentives.

They can tackle incentive problems by

- acknowledging that such problems exist.
- diagnosing the cause—hidden actions, hidden information, or badly designed incentives.
- creating or redesigning incentives that will induce partners to behave in ways that maximize the supply chain's profits.

They can redesign incentives by

• changing contracts to reward partners for acting in the supply chain's best interests.

• gathering or sharing information that was previously hidden.

• using intermediaries or personal relationships to develop trust with supply chain partners.

They can prevent incentive problems by

• conducting incentive audits when they adopt new technologies, enter new markets, or launch supply chain improvement programs.

• educating managers about processes and incentives at other companies in the supply chain.

• making discussions less personal by getting executives to examine problems at other companies or in other industries.

## The Economics of Incentive Alignment

IF A COMPANY ALIGNS the incentives of the firms in its supply chain, everyone will make higher profits. This isn't an idle claim; we can easily demonstrate it in the case of a two-company supply chain.

Let's say a publisher prints newspapers at a cost of 45 cents per copy and sells them to a news vendor for 80 cents each, and the newspaper retails for $1.00. Let's also assume that demand for the newspaper is uniformly distributed between 100 and 200 copies a day.

| Costs and Profits | Traditional Contract | Revenue-Sharing Contract | Markdown-Money Contract |
|---|---|---|---|
| Retail Price | $1.00 | $1.00 | $1.00 |
| Printing Cost | $0.45 | $0.45 | $0.45 |
| Wholesale Price | $0.80 | $0.45 | $0.80 |
| Vendor's Share of Revenue | 100% | 65% | 100% |
| Vendor's Compensation for Unsold Copies | — | — | $0.60 |
| Vendor's Understocking Cost | $0.20 | $0.20 | $0.20 |
| Vendor's Overstocking Cost | $0.80 | $0.45 | $0.20 |
| Inventory Level | 120 copies | 131 copies | 150 copies |
| Vendor's Daily Profit | $22.00 | $23.08 | $25.00 |
| Publisher's Daily Profit | $42.00 | $44.17 | $45.00 |
| Supply Chain's Daily Profit | $64.00 | $67.25 | $70.00 |

The vendor has to throw away unsold copies, so he has to compare two kinds of costs before deciding how many copies to stock. He loses 80 cents for every unsold copy, but if demand exceeds supply, his opportunity cost is 20 cents per copy. The vendor's inventory level will be optimal when the marginal understocking cost equals the marginal overstocking cost—in this case, when he orders 120 copies. The vendor will stock fewer copies than the average demand of 150 per day because the overstocking cost (80 cents) is four times higher than the understocking cost (20 cents). That could lead to frequent stock-outs.

If the publisher produced and sold the newspaper himself, he would incur an understocking cost of 55 cents (the retail price less the printing cost) and an overstocking cost of 45 cents (the unit cost of printing). According to our calculations, the publisher's profits would be greatest if he were to stock 155 copies, not 120. (For details on how we arrived at the numbers presented here, see V.G. Narayanan's technical note "The Economics of Incentive Alignment," Harvard Business School, 2004.) In fact, both the publisher and the consumers would be happier if there were more copies of the newspaper on the stands, but the vendor would not be. The vendor stocks less than everyone else would like him to because it is in his best interest to do so. The publisher therefore needs to change the incentives of the news vendor so that when the vendor chooses an inventory level that is in his best interest, it increases the publisher's profits.

One way the publisher could do that is by using a revenue-sharing contract and lowering the price the vendor pays for each copy from 80 cents to 45 cents. In return, the vendor could retain, say, 65% of the sale price and pass on 35% to the publisher. The retailer's understocking costs would remain 20 cents, but his overstocking costs would fall because he'd pay less for each copy. The retailer would now be inclined to stock 131 copies instead of 120. The profits of both the retailer and the publisher would rise (see the table).

Alternately, the publisher could pay the retailer markdown money of, let's suppose, 60 cents for every unsold copy. That would lower the overstocking cost of the retailer and encourage him to stock more copies. The publisher would more than make up for bearing some of that cost because of profits he'd gain in higher sales. In this case, the retailer would stock 150 copies.

As the exhibit shows, both the publisher and the retailer would earn more profits under the revenue-sharing and markdown-money contracts considered here than under the traditional system. The increase in profits would not come at the expense of consumers, who'd pay the same retail price. Inventory levels would also go up, which would result in greater consumer satisfaction.

**Originally published in November 2004**
**Reprint R0411F**

# About the Contributors

SCOTT BETH is the vice president of procurement at Intuit. At the time of the roundtable, Beth was a senior director of global sourcing for Agilent Technologies' electronic products and solutions group.

H. KENT BOWEN is the Bruce Rauner Professor of Business Administration at Harvard Business School.

DAVID N. BURT is a professor of supply chain management and the director of the University of San Diego's Institute of Supply Chain Management.

THOMAS Y. CHOI is a professor of supply chain management at the W.P. Carey School of Business at Arizona State University in Tempe.

WILLIAM COPACINO is the group chief executive of Accenture's Business Consulting capability group. He is the author of several books on supply chain management.

KASRA FERDOWS is the Heisley Family Professor of Global Manufacturing at Georgetown University's McDonough School of Business in Washington, D.C.

CHRIS GOPAL is the vice president of global supply chain management at Unisys. Previously he was the director of global supply chain consulting at Ernst & Young and a vice president at Dell Computer.

A. MICHAEL KNEMEYER is an assistant professor of logistics at Ohio State University's Fisher College of Business in Columbus.

DOUGLAS M. LAMBERT holds the Raymond E. Mason Chair in Transportation and Logistics at Ohio State University's Fisher College of Business in Columbus, and directs the Global Supply Chain Forum there.

HAU L. LEE is the Thoma Professor of Operations, Information, and Technology at Stanford University, co-director of the Stanford Global Supply Chain Management Forum, and director of the Managing Your Supply Chain for Global Competitiveness Executive Program.

MICHAEL A. LEWIS is a professor of operations and supply management at the University of Bath School of Management in the UK.

JEFFREY K. LIKER is a professor of industrial and operations engineering at the University of Michigan in Ann Arbor.

ROBERT PORTER LYNCH is the CEO of the Warren Company. He is the author of *Business Alliances Guide: The Hidden Competitive Weapon* (Wiley, 1993)

JOSE A.D. MACHUCA is a professor of operations management at the University of Seville in Spain.

SANDRA MORRIS is a vice president and the chief information officer of Intel, where she has been since 1985. Previously, she was at the David Sarnoff Research Center of RCA.

V.G. NARAYANAN is a professor of business administration at Harvard Business School in Boston.

ANANTH RAMAN is the UPS Foundation Professor of Business Logistics, at Harvard Business School in Boston.

STEVEN J. SPEAR is an assistant professor of business administration at Harvard Business School in Boston.

# Index